How to Become a Plumber

The Complete Guide to Plumbing Success

Mike Turner

Published by Fiel LLC, 2024.

While every precaution has been taken in the preparation of this book, the publisher assumes no responsibility for errors or omissions, or for damages resulting from the use of the information contained herein.

HOW TO BECOME A PLUMBER

First edition. November 13, 2024.

ISBN: 979-8230844747

Written by Mike Turner.

The Skilled Trade of Plumbing

The skilled trade of plumbing stands as one of civilization's most crucial yet often underappreciated professions. Since the dawn of human settlements, the need to transport water safely and efficiently has been paramount to public health and societal development. Today's plumbers are the torchbearers of this vital tradition, combining time tested techniques with modern technology to ensure our homes, businesses, and cities function smoothly.

At its core, plumbing encompasses far more than fixing leaky faucets or unclogging drains. It is a multifaceted profession that requires expertise in various systems, including water supply, drainage, venting, and gas distribution. Modern plumbers must understand complex building codes, work with diverse materials, and stay current with evolving technologies. They are problem solvers, critical thinkers, and skilled craftspeople who play an essential role in maintaining public health and safety.

The plumbing trade offers a unique combination of physical and mental challenges. On any given day, a plumber might need to diagnose mysterious leaks, calculate proper pipe sizing, interpret building plans, or devise creative solutions to unusual problems. This variety keeps the work interesting and ensures that no two days are exactly alike. The profession demands both technical knowledge and practical skills, making it an ideal career choice for those who enjoy hands on work while also wanting to engage their minds.

One of the most appealing aspects of the plumbing trade is its stability and growth potential. As long as buildings have water and waste systems, there will be a need for skilled plumbers. Unlike many modern careers that face uncertainty due to automation or outsourcing, plumbing requires physical presence and human expertise that cannot be replaced by technology. In fact, technological advances in the field have only increased the demand for knowledgeable professionals who can install and maintain increasingly sophisticated systems.

The path to becoming a plumber is well structured, though it requires dedication and patience. Most successful plumbers begin their careers through apprenticeship programs, which combine paid on the job training with classroom instruction. These programs typically last four to five years and cover everything from basic tool usage to advanced system design. During this time, apprentices work alongside experienced plumbers, gradually taking on more responsibility as they develop their skills.

Modern plumbing work encompasses several specialized areas, each with its own set of skills and certifications. Residential plumbers focus on homes and apartments, handling everything from routine maintenance to complete system installations. Commercial plumbers work on larger buildings and facilities, often dealing with more complex systems and stricter regulations. Industrial plumbers specialize in manufacturing facilities and process piping, while service and repair plumbers focus on maintaining and fixing existing systems.

The financial rewards of a plumbing career can be substantial. After completing an apprenticeship and obtaining necessary licenses, many plumbers earn well above the national average income. Those who start their own businesses or specialize in particular areas of the trade often have even greater earning potential. The trade also offers excellent benefits, including health insurance, retirement plans, and paid time off, particularly for those who join unions or work for established companies.

Beyond the financial aspects, plumbing offers the satisfaction of solving problems and helping people. Whether it's restoring water service during an emergency, protecting public health through proper sanitation, or helping homeowners save money through efficient systems, plumbers make a tangible difference in people's lives. This sense of purpose and accomplishment is a significant draw for many who enter the profession.

The plumbing trade is also evolving to meet modern challenges and opportunities. Green plumbing practices focus on water conservation and environmental sustainability. Smart home technology is creating new possibilities for water management and system monitoring. These developments are opening new specialties within the field and creating opportunities for plumbers to expand their expertise and services.

Safety and precision are paramount in plumbing work. Modern plumbers must understand and follow strict safety protocols to protect themselves and others. They must also be detail oriented, as even small mistakes can have serious consequences. This commitment to quality and safety is a fundamental aspect of the profession and requires ongoing education and awareness.

The plumbing community is typically tight knit and supportive, with experienced professionals often mentoring newcomers to the trade. Professional organizations, unions, and trade associations provide resources, training, and networking opportunities. This sense of community and shared purpose helps create a positive work environment and provides support throughout one's career.

As we move forward in this book, we'll explore each aspect of the plumbing profession in detail, from the basic tools and techniques to advanced systems and business management. Whether you're considering entering the trade, currently in training, or looking to advance your existing career, understanding these fundamentals is essential to success in the plumbing field. The journey to becoming a skilled plumber requires commitment and hard work, but the rewards both personal and professional make it a worthwhile pursuit for those drawn to this essential trade.

The History of Plumbing

The history of plumbing stretches back to the earliest human civilizations, but it was the Romans who truly revolutionized the art of water management and waste disposal. Their sophisticated aqueduct systems, lead pipe networks, and public bathhouses set standards that would influence plumbing practices for centuries to come. The Roman word "plumbum," meaning lead, gives us both the term "plumber" and the chemical symbol Pb, highlighting the ancient roots of this essential trade.

Following the fall of the Roman Empire, much of their plumbing knowledge was lost during the Dark Ages. Medieval Europe saw a significant regression in sanitation practices, leading to devastating consequences such as the spread of diseases like cholera and typhoid. It wasn't until the Renaissance that serious attention returned to the importance of proper sanitation and water management.

The Industrial Revolution marked a turning point in plumbing history. The rapid growth of cities created an urgent need for organized water supply and waste management systems. In 1804, Philadelphia became the first city to use cast iron pipes for its water system, setting a precedent that would soon be followed by other major urban centers. The development of indoor plumbing during this period represented a revolutionary improvement in public health and daily comfort.

The Victorian era brought significant advances in plumbing technology and sanitation awareness. Thomas Crapper, contrary to popular belief, didn't invent the flush toilet but did much to improve and popularize it through his plumbing company in London. The late 1800s saw the establishment of the first plumbing codes and the recognition of plumbing as a professional trade requiring specific skills and training.

The 20th century witnessed exponential growth in plumbing innovation. The development of new materials like copper piping in the 1930s provided alternatives to lead and cast iron. Plastic pipes, introduced in the 1950s, revolutionized the industry by offering lightweight, corrosion resistant, and cost effective solutions. Water heaters became commonplace, transforming the way people lived and leading to increased demand for skilled plumbers.

The standardization of plumbing practices became crucial during this period. Organizations like the American Society of Mechanical Engineers (ASME) and the American Society of Sanitary Engineering (ASSE) established guidelines that helped ensure consistency and safety across the industry. These standards continue to evolve, incorporating new technologies and addressing emerging challenges.

The advent of computer technology in the late 20th century brought new tools to the plumbing trade. Computer aided design (CAD) software allowed for more precise planning of plumbing systems, while diagnostic equipment became increasingly sophisticated. Video inspection cameras, introduced in the 1990s, revolutionized pipe inspection and maintenance procedures.

Environmental concerns began shaping plumbing practices in significant ways during the late 20th and early 21st centuries. The focus shifted toward water conservation, leading to the development of low flow fixtures and water efficient appliances. The removal of lead from plumbing systems became a priority, driven by increased awareness of its health risks.

Today's plumbing systems represent the culmination of thousands of years of technological evolution. Modern plumbers work with materials and tools their predecessors could hardly have imagined. Smart technology integration allows for remote monitoring of water usage and early leak detection. Greywater recycling systems and solar water heaters reflect growing environmental consciousness in the industry.

The basic principles of plumbing remain unchanged since ancient times: water must flow downhill, pressure must be managed, and systems must be properly vented. However, the methods and materials used to achieve these goals have become increasingly sophisticated. Modern plumbers must understand not only traditional techniques but also new technologies and environmental considerations.

The future of plumbing continues to evolve with emerging technologies. The Internet of Things (IoT) is creating opportunities for smart plumbing systems that can detect problems before they become serious. Water recycling and purification technologies are becoming more advanced, while new materials and installation techniques continue to be developed.

Looking back at the evolution of plumbing provides valuable context for today's practitioners. Understanding how the trade has developed helps inform current practices and anticipate future trends. From the Roman aqueducts to smart home integration, the history of plumbing reflects humanity's ongoing quest to manage water resources effectively and maintain public health.

The profession continues to adapt to new challenges, including water scarcity, environmental concerns, and changing building practices. As we face these challenges, the fundamental importance of skilled plumbing professionals remains constant. The evolution of plumbing from ancient times to the present day demonstrates both the enduring nature of its basic principles and its capacity for innovation and adaptation.

This rich history forms the foundation for modern plumbing practices, while pointing the way toward future developments. Today's plumbers stand as the latest in a long line of skilled craftspeople who have contributed to this essential trade, continuing to build upon and improve the techniques and technologies developed over thousands of years.

Choosing a Career in Plumbing

Choosing a career in plumbing offers numerous compelling advantages that make it an excellent choice for those seeking a stable, rewarding, and meaningful profession. Unlike many modern careers that face uncertainty due to automation and technological displacement, plumbing remains a field where human expertise and hands-on skills are irreplaceable. The fundamental need for clean water delivery and waste removal ensures that plumbers will always be in demand.

One of the most attractive aspects of pursuing a plumbing career is the ability to earn while you learn. Through apprenticeship programs, aspiring plumbers can begin earning a wage immediately while developing their skills under experienced mentors. This approach eliminates the burden of substantial student loan debt that often accompanies traditional college education, making it an financially prudent career choice for many young professionals.

The plumbing trade offers exceptional job security. Every building, whether residential or commercial, requires plumbing systems, and these systems need regular maintenance, repairs, and occasional replacement. Natural disasters, aging infrastructure, and new construction projects ensure a constant stream of work opportunities. Even during economic downturns, plumbing services remain essential, making the profession relatively recession proof.

Financial rewards in plumbing can be substantial. Licensed plumbers often earn well above the national average wage, with master plumbers and business owners having the potential to earn six figure incomes. The earning potential increases with experience, specialization, and the willingness to handle emergency calls or complex commercial projects. Additionally, many plumbers enjoy comprehensive benefits packages, including health insurance, retirement plans, and paid vacation time.

The variety of work available in plumbing keeps the career interesting and engaging. No two days are exactly alike, as plumbers encounter different challenges and situations with each job. From installing fixtures in new construction to troubleshooting complex problems in existing systems, the work requires both physical skills and mental agility. This diversity helps prevent the monotony that often accompanies desk bound occupations.

For those with entrepreneurial aspirations, plumbing provides excellent opportunities for business ownership. After gaining experience and proper licensing, many plumbers successfully establish their own companies. The relatively low overhead costs and constant demand for services make it an attractive business venture. Operating your own plumbing business allows for greater income potential and the satisfaction of building something from the ground up.

The trade also offers numerous paths for specialization and advancement. Plumbers can focus on residential service work, new construction, commercial projects, or industrial applications. They might choose to specialize in areas such as medical gas systems, fire suppression systems, or green plumbing technologies. These specializations often command premium rates and provide opportunities for continuous professional growth.

Personal satisfaction represents another compelling reason to choose plumbing as a career. Plumbers play a crucial role in maintaining public health and safety by ensuring clean water delivery and proper waste disposal. The ability to solve problems and help people in challenging situations provides a sense of accomplishment that many find deeply rewarding. Whether it's restoring water service during an emergency or completing a complex installation project, plumbers make a tangible difference in people's lives.

The physical nature of plumbing work appeals to those who enjoy staying active and working with their hands. Unlike sedentary office jobs, plumbing keeps you moving and engaged with your environment.

This physical activity, combined with mental problem solving, creates a satisfying balance that many find preferable to purely intellectual or purely physical work.

Technology integration in the plumbing field offers exciting opportunities for those interested in combining traditional skills with modern innovations. Smart home systems, water conservation technologies, and advanced diagnostic tools are becoming increasingly important in the trade. This evolution ensures that plumbers can continue to learn and adapt throughout their careers, keeping the work challenging and relevant.

The plumbing trade also provides excellent networking opportunities and a strong sense of community. Professional associations, trade shows, and continuing education programs allow plumbers to connect with colleagues, share knowledge, and stay current with industry developments. These connections can lead to business opportunities, mentorship relationships, and lasting professional friendships.

Environmental consciousness adds another dimension to the appeal of plumbing as a career. Modern plumbers play a vital role in promoting water conservation and implementing sustainable solutions. From installing water efficient fixtures to designing greywater systems, plumbers contribute significantly to environmental protection efforts. This aspect of the work resonates strongly with those who want their career to have a positive impact on the planet.

The structured nature of the career path, from apprentice to journeyman to master plumber, provides clear goals and benchmarks for professional development. This progression allows individuals to plan their career advancement and set achievable objectives. The certification and licensing requirements, while demanding, ensure high professional standards and respect for the trade.

Choosing plumbing as a career also means joining a profession with a rich history and proud traditions. Plumbers have been essential to human civilization for thousands of years, and this legacy continues today. The trade combines time tested principles with modern innovations, offering practitioners the opportunity to be part of both the heritage and future of this vital profession.

For those seeking a career that offers financial stability, personal satisfaction, and opportunities for growth, plumbing represents an excellent choice. The combination of technical skills, problem solving challenges, and essential service to society makes it a rewarding profession with enduring value.

Industry Growth and Demand

The plumbing industry continues to demonstrate robust growth and excellent income potential for skilled professionals. Current labor market analyses consistently show strong demand for qualified plumbers across residential, commercial, and industrial sectors, with this trend expected to continue well into the future. According to the Bureau of Labor Statistics, employment opportunities for plumbers are projected to grow faster than the average for all occupations, with tens of thousands of new positions opening annually.

Several factors contribute to this positive career outlook. The ongoing need to maintain, repair, and replace existing plumbing systems in aging buildings creates a steady stream of work. New construction projects, both residential and commercial, require skilled plumbers for initial installations. Additionally, stricter water efficiency standards and environmental regulations often necessitate system upgrades, creating further opportunities for plumbing professionals.

Salary expectations for plumbers vary based on experience level, geographic location, and specialization, but the earning potential is particularly attractive. Entry level apprentices typically start earning between 40 to 50 percent of what fully licensed plumbers make, with regular increases as they progress through their training. This starting wage often exceeds what many college graduates earn in their first jobs, and apprentices have the advantage of earning while learning without accumulating student debt.

Licensed journeyman plumbers consistently earn above average wages, with median annual salaries ranging from $45,000 to $75,000 in most regions. However, many plumbers earn significantly more, particularly those working in metropolitan areas or specializing in commercial or industrial projects. Master plumbers often command even higher salaries, with experienced professionals frequently earning well over $100,000 annually.

Overtime opportunities substantially increase earning potential in the plumbing field. Emergency calls, weekend work, and holiday service can command premium rates, often time and a half or double the standard hourly rate. Many plumbers strategically incorporate these higher paying opportunities into their schedules to maximize their income.

Geographic location plays a crucial role in determining earning potential. Urban areas and regions with high costs of living typically offer higher wages to compensate for increased living expenses. For example, plumbers working in major cities on either coast often earn significantly more than their counterparts in rural areas or smaller cities. However, this wage difference usually correlates with the local cost of living.

Specialization within the plumbing field can lead to enhanced earning potential. Plumbers who develop expertise in specific areas such as medical gas systems, fire suppression systems, or industrial process piping often command higher rates due to their specialized knowledge and skills. Similarly, those who become proficient in emerging technologies like smart home integration or sustainable water systems can differentiate themselves in the market and charge premium rates for their services.

Self employed plumbers and business owners have particularly high earning potential. While starting a plumbing business requires significant investment and involves additional risks, successful entrepreneurs can earn substantially more than employed plumbers. Business owners benefit from the ability to set their own rates, build a team, and scale their operations. Many successful plumbing business owners report annual revenues in the high six figures or even millions of dollars.

Benefits packages add significant value to plumber compensation, particularly for those working for established companies. Common benefits include health insurance, dental coverage, retirement plans, paid vacation time, and sick leave. Some employers also provide vehicle allowances, tool allowances, or continuing education reimbursement. These benefits can add thousands of dollars to the total compensation package.

Career advancement opportunities further enhance the long term financial outlook for plumbers. As professionals gain experience and additional certifications, they can move into supervisory roles, project management positions, or specialized technical roles. These advanced positions often come with increased salaries and additional benefits. Some plumbers transition into related fields such as plumbing inspection, teaching, or sales, where their practical experience is highly valued.

The stability of plumbing careers provides an additional financial advantage. Unlike many industries that experience significant fluctuations during economic downturns, plumbing services remain essential regardless of economic conditions. This stability allows plumbers to maintain steady income streams even during challenging economic times, contributing to long term financial security.

Union membership can significantly impact earning potential and benefits. Plumbers who belong to unions typically earn higher wages and receive more comprehensive benefits packages compared to non union workers. Union contracts often include provisions for regular wage increases, overtime protection, and enhanced retirement benefits. However, union opportunities vary by region and market conditions.

The future outlook for plumbing careers remains strong, with several factors suggesting continued growth in both demand and compensation. Increasing focus on water conservation, environmental sustainability, and energy efficiency creates new opportunities for plumbers with relevant expertise. The integration of technology into plumbing systems, including smart water management and automated monitoring systems, opens additional avenues for specialization and increased earning potential.

Demographic trends also support positive career prospects for plumbers. An aging workforce means many experienced plumbers will retire in the coming years, creating opportunities for advancement and increasing demand for new professionals entering the field. This generational transition is expected to maintain upward pressure on wages and benefits as employers compete for qualified workers.

When considering the career outlook and salary expectations for plumbers, it's important to recognize that success in the field requires ongoing commitment to professional development and excellence in service delivery. Those who invest in continuing education, maintain high quality standards, and build strong customer relationships typically achieve the best financial outcomes. The combination of strong demand, good wages, comprehensive benefits, and opportunities for advancement makes plumbing an attractive career choice for those willing to develop the necessary skills and work ethic.

Different Types of Plumbing Work

Different types of plumbing work encompass a broad spectrum of specialized services and applications, each requiring unique skills, knowledge, and expertise. Understanding these various specialties helps aspiring plumbers identify potential career paths and areas of focus within the trade.

Residential plumbing represents one of the most common types of plumbing work. This includes installation and maintenance of water supply lines, drain systems, and fixtures in homes. Residential plumbers work on everything from simple faucet repairs to complete bathroom remodels. They install and service water heaters, garbage disposals, dishwashers, and washing machines. Additionally, they handle emergency repairs such as burst pipes, clogged drains, and leaking fixtures that can cause significant damage if not addressed promptly.

Commercial plumbing involves working in office buildings, retail spaces, restaurants, and other business establishments. These projects typically involve larger scale systems and more complex installations than residential work. Commercial plumbers must understand specialized equipment like grease traps for restaurants, industrial grade water heaters, and large capacity drainage systems. They often work with different materials and larger pipe sizes than those commonly found in residential settings.

Industrial plumbing represents another significant sector within the field. Industrial plumbers work in manufacturing facilities, processing plants, and other industrial settings where specialized piping systems are crucial to operations. This type of work often involves installing and maintaining process piping systems that carry various liquids, gases, and sometimes chemicals used in manufacturing processes. Industrial plumbers must understand pressure systems, specialized materials, and complex industrial equipment.

New construction plumbing involves installing complete plumbing systems in newly built structures. This type of work requires careful planning and coordination with other trades, as plumbing systems must be integrated with the building's overall design and construction schedule. New construction plumbers read and interpret blueprints, plan pipe routing, and install systems according to local building codes and specifications.

Repair and maintenance plumbing forms a substantial portion of plumbing work. These plumbers respond to service calls for existing plumbing systems that need repair, replacement, or routine maintenance. This type of work requires strong diagnostic skills, as plumbers must identify problems and determine the most effective solutions. They often work in confined spaces and must be able to repair or replace components while minimizing disruption to existing structures.

Specialized plumbing services include areas like gas fitting, which involves installing and maintaining gas lines for appliances and heating systems. This work requires additional certifications and careful attention to safety protocols due to the hazardous nature of gas systems. Similarly, fire suppression system installation and maintenance represents another specialized area requiring specific certifications and expertise.

Green plumbing has emerged as an important specialty focusing on water conservation and environmental sustainability. These plumbers work with water efficient fixtures, greywater systems, solar water heaters, and other environmentally friendly technologies. They must stay current with evolving environmental regulations and new sustainable technologies entering the market.

Medical gas systems installation and maintenance represents a highly specialized type of plumbing work found in hospitals and medical facilities. This work involves installing and maintaining gas delivery systems for oxygen, nitrogen, and other medical gases. Due to the critical nature of these systems in healthcare settings, this specialty requires additional certifications and adherence to strict protocols.

Municipal plumbing work involves maintaining and repairing city water and sewer systems. These plumbers work on large scale infrastructure projects, including water main installation, sewer line maintenance, and storm water management systems. This type of work often requires heavy equipment operation and understanding of municipal infrastructure systems.

Plumbing design and engineering represents another specialized career path within the field. These professionals focus on designing plumbing systems for new construction projects, often working in conjunction with architects and engineers. They must understand complex calculations for water pressure, flow rates, and system capacity while ensuring compliance with building codes and regulations.

Pool and spa plumbing constitutes another distinct specialty. These plumbers install and maintain circulation systems, filters, heaters, and other components specific to pools and spas. They must understand water chemistry, filtration systems, and specialized equipment used in recreational water facilities.

Irrigation system installation and maintenance represents yet another specialized area within plumbing. These professionals work with outdoor water systems for lawns, gardens, and agricultural applications. They must understand water conservation principles, timing systems, and various irrigation technologies.

Each type of plumbing work presents its own challenges and opportunities for specialization. Many plumbers start their careers in residential or commercial work before developing expertise in specific areas. The diversity of available specialties allows plumbers to align their work with their interests and strengths while potentially increasing their earning potential through specialized knowledge and skills.

Success in any plumbing specialty requires ongoing education and adaptation to new technologies and techniques. As building systems become more complex and environmental concerns drive changes in plumbing practices, the need for specialized expertise continues to grow. Understanding the various types of plumbing work helps professionals make informed decisions about their career development and identify opportunities for growth within the field.

Commercial vs Residential Plumbing

Commercial and residential plumbing, while sharing many fundamental principles, represent distinct specialties within the plumbing trade, each with its own unique challenges, requirements, and opportunities. Understanding these differences is crucial for plumbers deciding which path to pursue in their careers.

Residential plumbing primarily focuses on homes and apartment buildings, where systems are generally smaller in scale but require a more personal touch with homeowners. Residential plumbers typically work with pipes ranging from half-inch to four inches in diameter, handling everything from simple fixture installations to complete home repiping projects. The work often involves direct interaction with homeowners, requiring strong customer service skills and the ability to explain complex problems in simple terms. Residential jobs frequently demand quick response times, especially for emergency situations like burst pipes or backed-up sewers that directly impact families' daily lives.

In contrast, commercial plumbing involves larger-scale systems found in office buildings, shopping centers, restaurants, and other business establishments. Commercial plumbers work with bigger pipe sizes, often ranging from two inches to twelve inches or larger in diameter. These systems must handle higher demands and more consistent usage patterns than residential systems. Commercial projects typically require more extensive planning and often involve coordinating with other construction trades and building managers.

The materials used in each sector can differ significantly. While residential plumbing commonly uses copper, PEX, or PVC pipes, commercial applications might require industrial-grade materials like cast iron, steel, or specialized alloys designed to handle higher pressures and more demanding conditions. Commercial systems also frequently incorporate more complex components like industrial water heaters, large-scale water filtration systems, and specialized waste management equipment.

Building codes and regulations present another significant difference between residential and commercial plumbing. Commercial buildings must meet stricter requirements for public safety, including more rigorous fire suppression systems, multiple backflow prevention devices, and enhanced ventilation systems. Commercial plumbers must maintain thorough knowledge of these regulations and ensure all installations meet current code requirements.

The work environment also varies considerably between residential and commercial plumbing. Residential plumbers typically work in occupied homes, requiring careful attention to cleanliness and minimal disruption of the household. They often work alone or in small teams, managing their own schedule of service calls throughout the day. Commercial plumbers, however, frequently work on construction sites or in business environments, coordinating with other trades and adhering to strict project timelines. Commercial jobs may require working during off-hours to minimize disruption to business operations.

Financial considerations differ between the two specialties as well. Residential plumbing often involves smaller, more frequent jobs with quicker payment cycles, typically from individual homeowners. Commercial projects tend to be larger in scope and budget but may involve longer payment terms and more complex billing procedures when working with property management companies or general contractors.

The tools and equipment required for each specialty can vary significantly. While both require basic hand tools and common power tools, commercial plumbing often necessitates additional specialized equipment like industrial drain cleaning machines, pipe threading equipment for larger diameter pipes, and heavy-duty lifting equipment.

Commercial plumbers might also need to be familiar with building automation systems and complex water management technologies.

Emergency response procedures differ between residential and commercial settings. Residential emergencies typically involve individual households and require immediate attention to prevent property damage and restore essential services. Commercial emergencies can affect hundreds of people and may require more complex solutions, often involving temporary systems to maintain business operations while repairs are completed.

The career progression paths in residential and commercial plumbing can also differ. Residential plumbers often advance by developing specialized skills in areas like bathroom remodeling or water heater installation, eventually perhaps starting their own service businesses. Commercial plumbers might progress into project management roles, overseeing large-scale installations or maintaining multiple properties for management companies.

Marketing and business development strategies vary between the two specialties. Residential plumbers often rely on word-of-mouth referrals, online reviews, and local advertising to build their customer base. Commercial plumbers typically develop relationships with general contractors, property managers, and facility maintenance companies to secure ongoing contracts and larger projects.

Training requirements can also differ significantly. While both specialties require comprehensive knowledge of basic plumbing principles, commercial plumbers often need additional certifications and training in areas like backflow prevention, medical gas systems, or industrial waste management. They might also need specialized safety training for working in commercial environments or with hazardous materials.

The scheduling and work-life balance aspects of each specialty present different challenges and opportunities. Residential plumbing often involves being on call for emergencies, with varying daily schedules based on service calls. Commercial plumbing might offer more predictable schedules, especially for maintenance contracts, but may require occasional evening or weekend work to accommodate business hours.

Understanding these differences helps plumbers make informed decisions about their career paths and specialization choices. Many successful plumbers gain experience in both areas before choosing to focus on one specialty or the other. Some maintain capabilities in both sectors, allowing them to adapt to market conditions and maximize their business opportunities. The choice between residential and commercial plumbing often depends on individual preferences, skills, and career goals, with each specialty offering unique opportunities for professional growth and success in the plumbing trade.

Physical Requirements and Work Environment

Physical requirements and work environment considerations are crucial aspects of a plumbing career that prospective professionals must carefully evaluate before entering the trade. The physical demands of plumbing work can be substantial, and understanding these requirements helps individuals prepare for and maintain long-term success in the field.

Plumbing is inherently a physically demanding profession that requires significant strength and endurance. On a typical day, plumbers frequently lift heavy materials and equipment, often weighing 50 pounds or more. Pipe sections, water heaters, fixtures, and tools must be transported to and from job sites and positioned correctly during installation. This constant heavy lifting necessitates proper technique and body mechanics to prevent injury and maintain long-term physical health.

The work environment frequently demands that plumbers maintain awkward positions for extended periods. Crawling through tight spaces, working under sinks, reaching overhead, and kneeling on hard surfaces are common daily activities. These positions can put strain on joints and muscles, particularly in the back, knees, and shoulders. Successful plumbers develop strategies to minimize physical stress, such as using knee pads, ergonomic tools, and proper positioning techniques.

Working conditions vary significantly depending on the job site and type of work being performed. Indoor environments might range from comfortable, climate-controlled spaces to cramped, poorly ventilated areas. Outdoor work exposes plumbers to various weather conditions, from extreme heat to bitter cold. Underground work in trenches or basements may involve exposure to moisture, dirt, and occasionally unpleasant conditions when dealing with sewage or waste systems.

Manual dexterity and hand-eye coordination are essential physical attributes for plumbers. The profession requires precise movements when working with tools, fitting pipes, and handling small components. Good vision is crucial for reading measurements, examining pipes for damage, and working with detailed blueprints. Some tasks may require color vision to distinguish between different types of pipes or wiring.

The physical demands extend beyond pure strength to include balance and stability. Plumbers often work on ladders, scaffolding, or in elevated positions. A good sense of balance and spatial awareness helps prevent accidents and ensures safe work practices. The ability to maintain steady hands while working with tools and performing precise measurements is also crucial for quality workmanship.

Environmental challenges in plumbing work can include exposure to various substances and conditions. Contact with chemicals, adhesives, and cleaning agents is common, requiring appropriate protective equipment and safety precautions. Plumbers may encounter asbestos in older buildings, requiring specialized safety protocols and certification for handling hazardous materials.

The profession demands significant stamina, as workdays can be long and physically taxing. Emergency calls may require extended hours or overnight work, particularly in severe weather conditions when pipe freezing and bursting are common. The ability to maintain focus and physical performance during long shifts is essential for both quality work and safety.

Noise exposure is another environmental consideration in plumbing work. Power tools, drilling, and other construction activities can create high noise levels, making hearing protection necessary. Similarly, dust and debris from cutting pipes or working in construction areas require appropriate respiratory protection and eye safety equipment.

The physical requirements of plumbing work necessitate a strong commitment to personal health and fitness. Regular exercise, particularly focusing on core strength and flexibility, can help plumbers maintain the physical capability needed for their work and prevent injuries. Proper nutrition and hydration are also important for maintaining energy levels throughout demanding workdays.

Adaptation to various work environments is a crucial skill for plumbers. One day might involve working in a pristine new construction site, while the next could require crawling through a muddy crawl space or working in an unfinished basement. The ability to adjust to these changing conditions while maintaining professional standards is essential.

Age considerations play a role in the physical aspects of plumbing work. While the trade can be practiced well into later years, many plumbers transition to supervisory or specialized roles that are less physically demanding as they age. Planning for this career evolution and maintaining physical health throughout one's career is important for long-term success.

The work environment also includes social aspects, as plumbers frequently interact with customers, other trades, and team members. Good communication skills and professional demeanor must be maintained even during physically challenging tasks. The ability to explain technical issues and propose solutions while possibly working in uncomfortable positions or adverse conditions is a valuable skill.

Technology is increasingly affecting the physical requirements and work environment of plumbing. New tools and equipment can help reduce physical strain, while diagnostic technologies may decrease the need for some manual inspections. However, the core physical demands of the profession remain significant, making it essential for plumbers to maintain their physical capabilities throughout their careers.

Understanding and preparing for these physical requirements and environmental conditions is crucial for anyone considering a plumbing career. Success in the field requires not just technical knowledge and skills, but also the physical capability and resilience to perform demanding work in varied conditions. Proper preparation, ongoing physical maintenance, and adherence to safety protocols help ensure a long and healthy career in the plumbing trade.

Essential Personal Qualities

Essential personal qualities for success in the plumbing trade extend far beyond technical skills and physical capabilities. These characteristics form the foundation of a plumber's professional identity and often determine their long-term success in the field.

Reliability stands as perhaps the most crucial personal quality for any plumber. Customers and employers depend on plumbers to arrive on time, complete work as promised, and respond promptly to emergencies. The nature of plumbing work, especially in crisis situations, demands professionals who can be counted on regardless of the hour or circumstances. This reliability must extend to every aspect of the job, from maintaining scheduled appointments to following through on commitments.

Problem solving ability ranks high among the essential traits for successful plumbers. Each job presents unique challenges that require creative thinking and analytical skills. A good plumber approaches each situation with methodical analysis, identifying the root cause of issues rather than just treating symptoms. This investigative mindset helps in diagnosing complex problems and developing effective solutions, often under pressure and with limited information.

Attention to detail cannot be overstated in its importance to plumbing work. Small oversights can lead to significant problems, from minor leaks to catastrophic failures. Successful plumbers maintain meticulous attention to every aspect of their work, from initial assessment through final testing. This quality ensures that installations are correct, repairs are thorough, and safety standards are consistently met.

Integrity and honesty form the bedrock of customer trust and professional reputation. Plumbers often work in people's homes and businesses, handling expensive equipment and making decisions that significantly impact their clients' properties. The ability to provide honest assessments, fair pricing, and ethical service recommendations builds long-term customer relationships and generates valuable referrals. This includes being forthright about one's capabilities and limitations, and never attempting work beyond one's expertise.

Adaptability proves essential in a field where no two days are exactly alike. Successful plumbers must adjust to different work environments, adapt to new technologies, and modify their approaches based on unique situation requirements. This flexibility extends to dealing with various personality types among customers, colleagues, and other trades professionals.

Communication skills play a vital role in plumbing success. The ability to explain complex technical issues in understandable terms helps customers make informed decisions about their plumbing needs. Clear communication also facilitates effective collaboration with team members, other trades, and regulatory officials. This includes both verbal and written communication, as documentation and record-keeping become increasingly important in the modern trade.

Patience serves as a valuable attribute when dealing with challenging situations. Complex problems may require time to properly diagnose and repair, while difficult customers or work conditions test one's composure. The ability to maintain a calm, professional demeanor under stress helps ensure quality work and positive customer relationships.

Time management skills prove crucial in balancing multiple jobs and priorities. Successful plumbers must efficiently schedule their work, estimate job durations accurately, and manage unexpected developments without compromising quality or customer service. This includes the ability to prioritize emergency calls while maintaining regular maintenance schedules.

Physical stamina combines with mental endurance in the plumbing trade. Beyond the obvious physical demands, plumbers must maintain focus and attention through long days, challenging conditions, and complex problem-solving situations. This mental toughness helps professionals persist through difficult jobs and maintain high standards regardless of circumstances.

Learning orientation marks successful plumbers throughout their careers. The field constantly evolves with new technologies, materials, and techniques. Those who embrace continuous learning and actively seek opportunities to expand their knowledge and skills position themselves for long-term success. This includes staying current with industry developments, pursuing additional certifications, and learning from both successes and failures.

Customer service orientation distinguishes exceptional plumbers in a competitive market. Understanding and responding to customer needs, maintaining professional appearance and demeanor, and following up after service completion build customer loyalty and business success. This includes the ability to manage customer expectations and handle complaints professionally.

Leadership qualities become increasingly important as plumbers advance in their careers. Whether managing apprentices, leading teams, or running their own businesses, the ability to guide and motivate others while maintaining high standards helps create successful long-term careers. This includes mentoring newer professionals and contributing to the overall development of the trade.

Initiative and self motivation drive successful plumbers to seek solutions, take on challenging projects, and continuously improve their skills. The ability to work independently, identify opportunities for improvement, and take action without constant supervision marks true professionals in the field.

These personal qualities combine to create plumbing professionals who not only excel technically but also build successful, sustainable careers. While some of these characteristics may come naturally, others can be developed through conscious effort and practice. Understanding and cultivating these essential qualities helps aspiring plumbers prepare for the challenges and opportunities ahead in their chosen profession.

The Role of Mathematics

Mathematics plays a fundamental role in the plumbing trade, serving as the foundation for many daily calculations and problem-solving tasks. While advanced calculus isn't necessary, plumbers must possess strong basic math skills to perform their work accurately and efficiently.

Measurement and conversion form the cornerstone of plumbing mathematics. Plumbers regularly work with both imperial and metric measurements, requiring fluency in converting between the two systems. This includes understanding fractions, decimals, and their relationships, as precise measurements are crucial for proper pipe fitting and system design. The ability to quickly convert between inches and millimeters, gallons and liters, or pounds per square inch and kilopascals proves essential in today's global industry.

Basic arithmetic serves plumbers constantly throughout their workday. Addition and subtraction come into play when calculating total pipe lengths, determining fitting allowances, or measuring distances between fixtures. Multiplication and division are necessary for scaling measurements, calculating flow rates, and determining pressure requirements. These fundamental operations must become second nature, as errors in basic calculations can lead to significant problems in system performance.

Geometry knowledge proves invaluable when working with piping systems. Understanding angles helps in planning pipe routes and calculating proper slopes for drainage. Area calculations become necessary when sizing water heaters, determining flow requirements, or planning bathroom layouts. Volume calculations help in sizing tanks, estimating water usage, and determining system capacity. The ability to visualize and work with three dimensional spaces helps plumbers plan efficient installations and troubleshoot existing systems.

Percentages and ratios appear frequently in plumbing calculations. Slope requirements for drain lines are typically expressed as percentages, such as the standard quarter inch per foot (approximately 2%) for waste lines. Understanding these relationships helps ensure proper drainage and system function. Ratios come into play when mixing chemicals, calculating ventilation requirements, or determining proper sizing for different parts of a system.

Basic algebra finds regular application in plumbing work. The ability to solve for unknown values using known variables helps in calculating pressure drops, determining flow rates, or sizing system components. While these calculations often use standard formulas and tables, understanding the underlying mathematical relationships helps plumbers adapt to unique situations and troubleshoot problems effectively.

Temperature calculations require comfort with both Fahrenheit and Celsius scales, as well as the ability to convert between them. This becomes particularly important when working with water heaters, checking system performance, or ensuring safe operating conditions. Understanding the relationship between temperature and pressure also proves crucial for many plumbing applications.

Estimating skills combine mathematical knowledge with practical experience. Plumbers must quickly and accurately estimate material quantities, labor time, and project costs. This requires not only basic calculation abilities but also the capacity to visualize completed projects and account for various factors that might affect the final requirements.

Financial mathematics becomes increasingly important as plumbers advance in their careers, particularly if they move into business ownership. Understanding markup, profit margins, overhead costs, and basic accounting principles helps ensure business success. The ability to calculate accurate quotes and manage project budgets relies heavily on mathematical competence.

Pipe sizing calculations incorporate multiple mathematical concepts. Factors such as flow rate, pressure loss, velocity, and friction must be considered when determining appropriate pipe diameters. While reference tables and modern software assist with these calculations, understanding the underlying mathematics helps plumbers make informed decisions and verify results.

The advent of digital tools and calculators hasn't diminished the importance of mental math skills in plumbing. The ability to quickly perform basic calculations and estimate measurements in the field saves time and helps identify potential errors before they become problems. Strong mental math skills also enhance professional credibility when discussing projects with customers or other trades.

Water pressure calculations require understanding the relationship between height, pressure, and flow. The concept that every 2.31 feet of height creates one pound per square inch of pressure forms the basis for many plumbing calculations. This knowledge helps in designing systems, troubleshooting pressure problems, and ensuring adequate water supply throughout buildings.

Plumbers must also understand mathematical concepts related to expansion and contraction of materials. Temperature changes cause pipes and fittings to expand or contract, requiring careful calculation of allowances and proper installation techniques. These calculations help prevent damage and ensure system longevity.

The importance of accuracy in plumbing mathematics cannot be overstated. Small errors in calculation can lead to significant problems in system performance, wasted materials, or safety concerns. Developing strong mathematical skills and habits of double checking calculations helps prevent costly mistakes and ensures professional quality work.

For aspiring plumbers who feel uncertain about their mathematical abilities, numerous resources exist for improvement. Trade schools and apprenticeship programs typically include focused instruction on plumbing mathematics. Additional practice through online resources, workbooks, or adult education courses can help build confidence and competence in essential mathematical skills.

Understanding Building Codes and Regulations

Building codes and regulations form the essential framework that ensures plumbing systems are installed safely and function properly. Every plumber must develop a thorough understanding of these requirements, as they govern virtually every aspect of the trade and exist to protect public health and safety.

The history of plumbing codes traces back to the early 20th century when cities began implementing standardized requirements in response to public health concerns. Today, most jurisdictions in the United States base their regulations on model codes such as the International Plumbing Code (IPC) or the Uniform Plumbing Code (UPC), though specific requirements can vary significantly between locations.

These codes establish minimum standards for everything from pipe sizing and material selection to installation methods and system design. They specify required distances between fixtures, proper venting configurations, acceptable slope ranges for drain lines, and countless other technical details that ensure plumbing systems function safely and effectively. Learning these requirements takes time and dedication, as the relevant code books often contain thousands of pages of detailed specifications.

Water supply regulations focus on preventing contamination and ensuring safe drinking water. This includes requirements for proper backflow prevention, specifications for pipe materials that can carry potable water, and rules about cross connections between potable and non potable systems. The code also establishes minimum pressure requirements and sizing guidelines to ensure adequate water supply throughout buildings.

Drainage system regulations address both sanitary and storm drainage requirements. These include specifications for proper pipe sizing, minimum slope requirements, cleanout placement, and venting configurations. The code also establishes requirements for grease interceptors, oil separators, and other specialized equipment needed in commercial applications. Understanding these requirements proves crucial for designing and installing systems that effectively remove waste while protecting public health.

Venting requirements ensure proper system operation and protect against dangerous sewer gases entering buildings. The code specifies minimum vent sizes, maximum distances between fixtures and vents, and acceptable configurations for various situations. These requirements can be particularly complex, as proper venting depends on multiple factors including fixture unit loads, developed length of pipe runs, and building configuration.

Fixture requirements establish minimum standards for installation and performance of plumbing fixtures like toilets, sinks, and water heaters. This includes specifications for water consumption, installation clearances, accessibility requirements, and proper connection methods. The Americans with Disabilities Act (ADA) adds another layer of requirements for commercial installations, ensuring facilities are accessible to all users.

Material requirements specify which types of pipe and fittings can be used for different applications. This includes limitations on materials for specific uses, requirements for protection against physical damage, and specifications for proper support and anchoring. Understanding these requirements helps plumbers select appropriate materials that will provide long term reliability while meeting code requirements.

Testing requirements establish procedures for verifying system integrity before use. This includes pressure testing of water supply lines, leak testing of drain systems, and inspection of completed installations.

Knowledge of these requirements helps plumbers plan their work efficiently and ensure installations will pass inspection the first time.

Local amendments to model codes can significantly affect requirements in specific jurisdictions. Plumbers must stay informed about these local variations, as they may be more stringent than base code requirements or address specific regional concerns. This might include special requirements for earthquake protection in seismic zones or enhanced freeze protection in cold climates.

Permit requirements vary by jurisdiction but typically specify when permits are needed and what documentation must be provided. Understanding these requirements helps plumbers properly plan projects and avoid potential legal issues. This includes knowing when engineered drawings are required and what level of detail must be provided for permit applications.

Safety requirements extend beyond basic plumbing function to address issues like proper ventilation, protection of potable water, and prevention of scalding. The code establishes maximum hot water temperatures for various applications and requires specific safety devices in certain situations. Understanding these requirements helps plumbers protect both themselves and their customers.

Code enforcement varies by jurisdiction but typically involves regular inspections during installation. Developing good relationships with local inspectors while maintaining strict compliance with all requirements helps ensure smooth project completion. This includes understanding common inspection points and maintaining proper documentation of all work performed.

The complexity of modern building codes requires plumbers to continually update their knowledge. Regular code changes incorporate new technologies and address emerging concerns, making ongoing education essential. Professional organizations and local authorities often provide training on code updates and interpretations.

Violations of plumbing codes can result in serious consequences including fines, required remediation work, and potential liability issues. Understanding and following code requirements protects plumbers professionally while ensuring the safety and satisfaction of their customers. This makes thorough knowledge of applicable codes and regulations one of the most valuable assets a plumber can possess.

Starting Your Career: Education and Training

When pursuing a career in plumbing, one of the first major decisions you'll need to make is choosing between attending a trade school program or seeking a direct apprenticeship. Both paths can lead to success in the field, but they offer different advantages and challenges that should be carefully considered based on your specific circumstances and learning style.

Trade schools, also known as vocational schools or technical colleges, provide structured classroom education combined with hands-on training in a controlled environment. These programs typically last between six months and two years, offering students a foundation in plumbing theory, mathematics, blueprint reading, and basic practical skills before they enter the workforce. The controlled learning environment allows students to make mistakes and learn from them without the pressure of a real job site, and instructors can provide immediate feedback and correction.

The curriculum in trade schools is carefully designed to cover all essential aspects of the trade systematically. Students learn about tools, materials, installation techniques, and safety protocols through a combination of classroom instruction and laboratory work. Many programs also include courses in business practices, customer service, and local building codes, providing a well-rounded education that prepares graduates for various aspects of the profession.

Direct apprenticeships, on the other hand, offer immediate immersion in real-world plumbing work. Apprentices learn primarily through on-the-job training under the supervision of experienced plumbers, supplemented by required classroom instruction typically provided through union programs or employer associations. This approach allows apprentices to earn while they learn, gaining practical experience from day one and developing professional relationships within the industry.

The financial considerations between these two paths can be significant. Trade school programs require upfront tuition payments and may necessitate student loans, though they often take less time to complete than traditional apprenticeships. Direct apprenticeships generally have minimal educational costs, and apprentices earn wages that typically increase as they gain experience and skills. However, starting wages for apprentices are usually quite low, reflecting their initial lack of skills and experience.

One advantage of trade school programs is the structured learning environment that ensures comprehensive coverage of fundamental concepts. Students benefit from dedicated instructors who can explain complex topics in detail and provide individual attention when needed. The classroom setting also allows for more theoretical discussion and understanding of the scientific principles behind plumbing systems, which can be valuable when troubleshooting complex problems later in one's career.

Trade schools often maintain relationships with local employers and may offer job placement assistance to graduates. Many programs include internship opportunities that can lead to full-time employment, and some schools have articulation agreements with apprenticeship programs that allow graduates to enter with advanced standing. The networking opportunities available through trade schools can be valuable for launching your career.

Direct apprenticeships offer the advantage of immediate practical experience and exposure to real-world situations. Apprentices learn to work efficiently under actual job conditions, develop problem-solving skills through hands-on experience, and become familiar with the physical demands of the trade. They also learn important soft skills like customer service and job site communication through direct interaction with clients and other trades.

The length of training varies between the two paths. Trade school programs typically offer more concentrated education over a shorter period, while apprenticeships usually last four to five years. However, trade school graduates often still need to complete an apprenticeship period, though it may be shortened based on their prior education. The total time to reach journeyman status may be similar regardless of the initial path chosen.

Some individuals choose to combine both approaches, completing a trade school program before entering an apprenticeship. This can provide a strong theoretical foundation while still gaining the benefits of extensive hands-on training. The trade school education may make the apprenticeship period more productive and could lead to faster advancement.

The choice between trade school and direct apprenticeship often depends on individual circumstances, learning style, and local opportunities. Factors to consider include your financial situation, preferred learning environment, availability of programs in your area, and long-term career goals. Some regions may have more opportunities for one path over the other, and local union requirements can also influence the decision.

Both paths require dedication and hard work to succeed. Trade school students must maintain good academic standing while developing practical skills, and apprentices must prove their worth on the job while completing required classroom instruction. Either way, the end goal remains the same: becoming a skilled, licensed plumber capable of performing quality work safely and efficiently.

The evolution of the plumbing industry, with new technologies and techniques constantly emerging, means that either educational path should be viewed as just the beginning of a career-long learning process. Successful plumbers, regardless of their initial training path, commit to continuous education and skill development throughout their careers.

Finding Apprenticeship Programs

Finding and applying for apprenticeship programs is a crucial step in beginning your plumbing career. The process requires careful research, preparation, and persistence, but with the right approach, you can secure a position that will launch your journey in the trade.

The first step in finding apprenticeship opportunities is to research the programs available in your area. Apprenticeships are typically offered through local unions, non union contractors, and independent plumbing companies. The United Association of Journeymen and Apprentices of the Plumbing and Pipe Fitting Industry (UA) operates many apprenticeship programs throughout North America. State and local plumbing associations also frequently maintain lists of available apprenticeship opportunities.

Before beginning your search, ensure you meet the basic requirements for apprenticeship programs. Most require candidates to be at least 18 years old, have a high school diploma or equivalent, possess a valid driver's license, and be physically capable of performing the work. Some programs may require a clean drug test and background check. Having basic math skills and mechanical aptitude will strengthen your application.

When applying for apprenticeship programs, proper documentation is essential. You'll typically need to provide your high school transcripts, proof of any relevant coursework or certifications, and multiple forms of identification. Some programs may require letters of recommendation from previous employers or teachers. Having these documents organized and readily available will help streamline the application process.

Union apprenticeship programs often have specific application windows during the year. These periods may only open briefly, sometimes for as little as a week or two, so it's important to stay informed about application deadlines. Many local unions maintain websites or hotlines with information about application periods. Signing up for notifications or regularly checking these resources can help ensure you don't miss opportunities.

The application process for union apprenticeships typically involves several steps. After submitting your initial application, you may be required to take an aptitude test covering math and reading comprehension. If you pass the test, you'll likely be invited for an interview with the apprenticeship committee. This interview is crucial, as it allows the committee to assess your attitude, work ethic, and commitment to the trade.

Non union contractors and independent plumbing companies may have more flexible application processes. Many accept applications year round and may be more willing to take on apprentices with limited experience. However, these opportunities can be more challenging to find, as they're often not as well advertised as union programs. Networking within the industry, attending trade shows, and directly contacting plumbing companies can help uncover these opportunities.

When preparing for apprenticeship interviews, research the program and company thoroughly. Understanding their history, values, and expectations demonstrates genuine interest and preparation. Be ready to discuss why you want to become a plumber, your long term career goals, and any relevant experience or skills you possess. Professional appearance and punctuality are essential for making a good impression.

Many successful applicants improve their chances by gaining related experience before applying. This might include taking basic plumbing courses at a technical school, working in construction or maintenance, or completing safety certifications. While not always required, such experience demonstrates initiative and familiarity with the construction environment.

The competition for apprenticeship positions can be intense, particularly in union programs. Don't be discouraged if you're not accepted on your first attempt. Use any feedback received to strengthen future applications. Some applicants find success by applying to multiple programs or considering opportunities in neighboring regions.

Once accepted into an apprenticeship program, you'll need to complete necessary paperwork and possibly pay initial fees. Union programs typically require members to pay dues and may have other associated costs. Some programs require apprentices to purchase their own basic tools before starting. Understanding these requirements in advance allows for proper financial planning.

It's important to maintain a professional attitude throughout the application process. Follow up appropriately after submitting applications and attending interviews, but avoid being overly aggressive. Remember that the plumbing industry values reliability and professionalism, and these qualities should be evident in your interactions during the application process.

Many apprenticeship programs maintain waiting lists, even after accepting qualified candidates. If placed on a waiting list, stay in contact with the program coordinator and use the waiting period productively. This might include taking relevant courses, obtaining additional certifications, or gaining experience in related fields.

Successful apprenticeship applicants often demonstrate not just technical potential but also soft skills like communication, teamwork, and problem solving ability. During interviews and interactions with program coordinators, highlight experiences that showcase these qualities. Examples might include team sports participation, leadership roles, or previous customer service experience.

The apprenticeship application process requires patience and persistence, but the reward is entry into a stable and rewarding career. By thoroughly researching opportunities, preparing comprehensive applications, and maintaining a professional approach, you can position yourself as a strong candidate for plumbing apprenticeship programs.

The Licensing Process

Beginning your apprenticeship marks an exciting and challenging phase in your journey to becoming a professional plumber. During this period, typically lasting four to five years, you'll experience a comprehensive combination of classroom instruction and hands on training that will form the foundation of your career.

The first year of apprenticeship often focuses on basic skills and safety protocols. You'll spend considerable time learning to identify and properly use hand tools and power equipment. Many apprentices are surprised by the amount of cleanup and preparation work involved in their early days. This is an intentional part of the learning process, allowing you to observe experienced plumbers while becoming familiar with job site operations and safety requirements.

Your daily routine as an apprentice will typically involve working alongside journeyman plumbers, helping with tasks of increasing complexity as your skills develop. Early morning start times are common in the plumbing trade, with many crews beginning work at 6:00 or 7:00 AM. You'll need to adjust your schedule accordingly and ensure reliable transportation to various job sites.

Classroom instruction forms a crucial component of your apprenticeship. Most programs require approximately 144 hours of classroom training each year, often scheduled during evenings or weekends. These sessions cover essential theoretical knowledge, including mathematics, physics, chemistry, and local plumbing codes. You'll learn about water distribution systems, drainage principles, venting requirements, and building regulations.

Financial considerations during apprenticeship are important to understand. While apprentices earn wages from the start, the initial pay typically begins at 40 to 50 percent of a journeyman's rate. Your wages will increase incrementally as you progress through the program, usually with raises every six months to one year based on your performance and accumulated hours. Many apprentices find it beneficial to budget carefully during these early years, considering that they may need to purchase tools and pay for educational materials.

The physical demands of apprenticeship can be significant. You'll spend long hours on your feet, often working in confined spaces or awkward positions. Heavy lifting, climbing ladders, and working in various weather conditions are common requirements. Maintaining good physical condition and practicing proper ergonomics becomes essential for long term success in the trade.

Throughout your apprenticeship, you'll be evaluated regularly on both your practical skills and theoretical knowledge. These assessments help track your progress and identify areas needing improvement. Many programs require apprentices to maintain detailed logs of their work hours and types of tasks performed, which must be verified by their supervising journeyman.

One of the most valuable aspects of apprenticeship is the opportunity to learn from experienced plumbers. Pay close attention to not just the technical aspects of their work, but also how they interact with customers, solve problems, and manage time efficiently. Many successful plumbers credit their apprenticeship mentors with teaching them crucial aspects of the trade that aren't found in textbooks.

Safety training remains a constant focus throughout your apprenticeship. You'll learn about proper personal protective equipment, job site hazards, safe tool operation, and emergency procedures. Many programs include specific certifications for areas like confined space entry, fall protection, and first aid.

As you progress through your apprenticeship, you'll gradually take on more complex tasks under supervision. This might include installing fixtures, troubleshooting problems, reading blueprints, and planning basic installations. The level of responsibility increases as you demonstrate competence and reliability.

Communication skills develop significantly during apprenticeship. You'll learn to effectively convey technical information to customers, coordinate with other trades on construction sites, and document your work accurately. Many apprentices find that developing strong professional relationships during this period leads to valuable connections throughout their careers.

Technology plays an increasingly important role in modern plumbing, and your apprenticeship will likely include training on various digital tools and equipment. This might include electronic diagnostic devices, computer aided design software, and digital documentation systems. Staying current with technological advances becomes an important aspect of your professional development.

The final years of apprenticeship often focus on more specialized skills and preparation for licensing exams. You'll gain experience with complex systems, learn advanced troubleshooting techniques, and develop the confidence to work more independently. Many apprentices begin to identify areas of specialization they might want to pursue in their future careers.

Remember that every apprentice's experience is unique, influenced by factors like location, type of program, and the specific focus of their employer. Some may spend more time on new construction, while others primarily work on service and repair. This diversity of experience helps create well rounded professionals capable of handling various plumbing challenges.

Success during apprenticeship requires dedication, patience, and a strong work ethic. There will be challenging days and difficult tasks, but maintaining a positive attitude and willingness to learn will help you make the most of this valuable training period. The skills and knowledge gained during apprenticeship create the foundation for a rewarding career in the plumbing trade.

Essential Plumbing Tools

Working with a master plumber represents one of the most valuable learning opportunities in your plumbing career. Master plumbers have typically accumulated at least seven to ten years of experience beyond their journeyman certification and have demonstrated exceptional proficiency in all aspects of the trade. Their extensive knowledge and practical wisdom provide an invaluable resource for developing plumbers at all levels.

Master plumbers often serve as primary mentors during the apprenticeship phase and continue to guide journeymen as they advance in their careers. They possess not only technical expertise but also a deep understanding of problem solving approaches that can only come from years of hands on experience. When working alongside a master plumber, you'll observe how they analyze complex situations, develop innovative solutions, and maintain high standards of workmanship.

The relationship between a master plumber and those working under their supervision requires mutual respect and clear communication. Master plumbers are responsible for ensuring that all work meets code requirements and professional standards. They often delegate tasks based on their assessment of each team member's skill level and readiness for new challenges. This measured approach to skill development helps prevent costly mistakes while building confidence in less experienced plumbers.

One of the most significant benefits of working with a master plumber is gaining exposure to their decision making process. Master plumbers frequently encounter situations that require quick thinking and creative problem solving. They draw upon their vast experience to evaluate multiple solutions, considering factors such as cost effectiveness, long term durability, and client satisfaction. Observing how they navigate these challenges provides invaluable lessons in professional judgment.

Master plumbers also play a crucial role in teaching advanced technical skills. They often specialize in complex systems or particular types of installations that require additional expertise. This might include medical gas systems, industrial process piping, or specialized water treatment facilities. Working alongside them on these projects provides exposure to advanced techniques and specialized equipment that you might not encounter in routine residential or commercial work.

Safety oversight represents another critical function of master plumbers. Their experience allows them to anticipate potential hazards and implement appropriate preventive measures. They understand not only the immediate safety concerns but also the long term implications of various installation methods and material choices. This comprehensive approach to safety helps create a culture of responsible work practices throughout their teams.

Business management skills often distinguish master plumbers from other professionals in the field. Many operate their own companies or hold senior positions in larger organizations. They understand project estimation, client relations, regulatory compliance, and team management. Working closely with a master plumber provides insights into these business aspects of the trade, which becomes particularly valuable if you aspire to run your own plumbing business in the future.

Master plumbers frequently serve as liaisons between various stakeholders on large projects. They coordinate with architects, engineers, building officials, and other trades to ensure smooth project execution. Observing these interactions helps develop the professional communication skills necessary for career advancement. You'll learn how to effectively discuss technical issues with both industry professionals and clients who may have limited plumbing knowledge.

The teaching style of master plumbers often reflects their own learning experiences and professional philosophy. Some prefer a hands on approach, demonstrating techniques and then closely supervising practice attempts. Others may emphasize theoretical understanding before practical application. Regardless of their teaching method, successful master plumbers share a commitment to maintaining high standards and fostering professional growth in their team members.

Documentation and record keeping practices often receive special attention from master plumbers. They understand the importance of maintaining accurate records for regulatory compliance, warranty purposes, and business operations. Working under their supervision, you'll learn proper procedures for documenting installations, repairs, and maintenance work. This attention to detail becomes increasingly important as you take on more responsibility in your career.

Master plumbers often maintain connections with manufacturers, suppliers, and industry organizations. These relationships help them stay informed about new products, evolving technologies, and changes in building codes. Their involvement in professional networks can provide valuable opportunities for those working under their supervision to expand their own industry connections and access continuing education resources.

The mentorship of a master plumber extends beyond technical skills to include professional ethics and customer service. They understand that reputation and trust are essential elements of a successful plumbing career. Through their example, you'll learn how to handle difficult client situations, maintain professional boundaries, and build long term business relationships.

Working with different master plumbers throughout your career can expose you to various specializations and approaches within the trade. Each master plumber brings unique experiences and expertise that contribute to your professional development. This diversity of knowledge helps create well rounded professionals capable of handling a wide range of plumbing challenges.

Remember that the relationship with a master plumber is a two way street. While they provide guidance and share their knowledge, they also expect dedication, reliability, and a willingness to learn from those working under their supervision. Demonstrating these qualities helps build trust and often leads to increased responsibilities and learning opportunities.

Advanced Tools for Specialized Work

The journeyman phase represents a critical transition in a plumber's career, marking the period between completing an apprenticeship and potentially advancing to master plumber status. As a journeyman plumber, you've demonstrated sufficient knowledge and skills to work independently, yet continue developing expertise through hands on experience with increasingly complex projects.

During this phase, which typically lasts several years, journeyman plumbers take on greater responsibility while still operating under the general supervision of master plumbers. They begin managing their own service calls, troubleshooting problems independently, and often supervising apprentices on job sites. This increased autonomy allows journeymen to build confidence in their decision making abilities and develop their own approach to problem solving.

The daily work of a journeyman plumber varies significantly depending on their employer and specialization. Some focus primarily on new construction, working with blueprints and installing complete plumbing systems in residential or commercial buildings. Others concentrate on service and repair work, responding to emergency calls and maintaining existing systems. Many journeymen gain experience in both areas, making them more versatile professionals.

One of the most significant aspects of the journeyman phase involves developing project management skills. Journeymen must learn to estimate time and materials accurately, coordinate with other trades, and ensure work progresses efficiently. They become responsible for ordering supplies, maintaining inventory on their service vehicles, and documenting their work thoroughly. These organizational skills prove essential for career advancement and eventual business ownership.

Customer service becomes increasingly important during the journeyman phase. While apprentices might have limited client interaction, journeymen regularly communicate with property owners, contractors, and building officials. They must explain technical issues clearly, provide accurate cost estimates, and maintain professional relationships. This aspect of the work often distinguishes successful journeymen from those who struggle to advance in their careers.

Technical expertise continues to expand during the journeyman phase through exposure to diverse challenges and systems. Journeymen encounter unusual problems that require creative solutions, work with new products and technologies, and adapt to evolving industry standards. Many choose to pursue additional certifications or specialized training to enhance their capabilities and market value.

Code compliance and inspection procedures become second nature during this period. Journeymen must thoroughly understand local building codes and maintain awareness of regulatory changes. They learn to anticipate potential inspection issues and ensure their work exceeds minimum requirements. This attention to detail helps build positive relationships with building officials and reduces costly callbacks.

The journeyman phase often includes opportunities to mentor apprentices, providing valuable leadership experience. Teaching others helps reinforce technical knowledge and develops communication skills. Many journeymen discover they enjoy the teaching aspect of their work, which can influence their future career choices within the industry.

Financial awareness typically increases during the journeyman phase as plumbers begin understanding the business aspects of their trade. They learn to balance quality with cost effectiveness, recognize opportunities for upselling appropriate services, and appreciate the importance of efficient work practices. This business acumen becomes particularly valuable for those planning to establish their own companies.

Safety responsibilities expand significantly for journeyman plumbers. They must not only ensure their own safety but also monitor working conditions for apprentices and other team members. Understanding and implementing proper safety protocols becomes especially critical when working with hazardous materials or in confined spaces. Journeymen often participate in developing safety procedures and conducting training sessions.

During this phase, many plumbers begin specializing in particular aspects of the trade that interest them or offer strong market opportunities. Some focus on medical gas systems, others on industrial processes, and still others on residential service work. This specialization often influences their choice of continuing education and their long term career trajectory.

The journeyman phase typically lasts between four and seven years, though this varies by jurisdiction and individual circumstances. During this time, plumbers accumulate the experience hours required for master plumber certification while developing the comprehensive knowledge base necessary for advanced licensure examinations.

Networking becomes increasingly important during the journeyman phase. Professional relationships developed during this period often lead to future business opportunities or career advancement. Many journeymen join trade associations, attend industry events, and build connections with suppliers and manufacturers. These relationships provide valuable resources for problem solving and staying current with industry developments.

Time management skills reach new levels of importance as journeymen balance multiple projects and responsibilities. They learn to prioritize emergency calls, maintain scheduled maintenance appointments, and coordinate with other trades on construction projects. Effective time management directly impacts customer satisfaction and profitability.

The journeyman phase represents a period of significant professional growth and development. Success during this time requires dedication to continuous learning, strong work ethic, and commitment to quality craftsmanship. Those who make the most of this phase position themselves well for advancement to master plumber status or successful business ownership.

Safety Equipment and Practices

State licensing requirements represent a crucial milestone in every plumber's career path, establishing the legal framework that governs professional practice in the plumbing industry. Each state maintains its own specific requirements for plumbing licensure, though many common elements exist across jurisdictions. Understanding these requirements is essential for anyone pursuing a career in plumbing.

Most states require plumbers to obtain licenses at multiple levels, typically including apprentice, journeyman, and master plumber classifications. The initial apprentice license or registration usually requires minimal prerequisites beyond age requirements and sometimes a high school diploma or equivalent. This entry level credential allows individuals to begin working under supervision while learning the trade.

The requirements for journeyman licensure become significantly more rigorous. States typically mandate completion of a registered apprenticeship program or equivalent combination of classroom instruction and supervised work experience. This usually translates to approximately 8,000 hours of documented work experience, typically accumulated over four to five years. Additionally, most jurisdictions require completion of related technical instruction, often totaling 576 to 744 classroom hours covering plumbing theory, mathematics, safety protocols, and code requirements.

Master plumber licensing requirements represent the highest level of credentialing in most states. Candidates must usually demonstrate several years of experience working as a licensed journeyman plumber, typically ranging from two to five years depending on the jurisdiction. Some states require additional classroom instruction or specialized training for master plumber candidates. The experience requirements ensure that only seasoned professionals with comprehensive knowledge of the trade can achieve this advanced certification.

Documentation plays a vital role in the licensing process across all levels. States require detailed records of work experience, often including signed affidavits from supervising plumbers verifying the types of work performed and hours accumulated. Educational transcripts, completion certificates from approved training programs, and documentation of continuing education credits must be maintained and submitted as required by state licensing boards.

Criminal background checks have become standard requirements for plumbing licensure in many states. These screenings help protect public safety and maintain professional standards within the industry. Some jurisdictions may restrict licensing based on certain criminal convictions, particularly those involving fraud or violent offenses. Applicants should research their state's specific policies regarding background checks and any potential disqualifying factors.

Insurance and bonding requirements vary significantly by state and license classification. Many jurisdictions require licensed plumbers to maintain minimum levels of liability insurance and sometimes performance bonds. These financial requirements protect both consumers and plumbers by providing coverage for potential damages or disputes arising from plumbing work. Master plumbers who operate their own businesses often face additional insurance requirements.

Continuing education represents an ongoing licensing requirement in most states. Licensed plumbers must typically complete a specified number of approved training hours during each renewal period to maintain their credentials. These requirements ensure that practitioners stay current with evolving technology, code changes, and industry best practices. States often mandate that a portion of continuing education focus on specific topics such as safety regulations or code updates.

Reciprocity agreements between states can affect licensing requirements for plumbers who relocate or work across state lines. While some states maintain reciprocal licensing arrangements that recognize credentials from other jurisdictions, many require plumbers to meet additional requirements or pass state specific examinations before granting licenses. Understanding these agreements becomes particularly important for plumbers working in metropolitan areas that span multiple states.

Application fees and renewal costs constitute another aspect of licensing requirements that varies by state and credential level. Initial licensing fees typically range from several hundred to over a thousand dollars, with renewal fees generally being somewhat lower. Some states require annual renewals, while others operate on two or three year cycles. Plumbers must factor these ongoing costs into their career planning and business operations.

Code knowledge requirements feature prominently in state licensing regulations. Most jurisdictions adopt specific plumbing codes, often based on the International Plumbing Code or Uniform Plumbing Code, but frequently modified with state specific amendments. Licensed plumbers must demonstrate thorough understanding of applicable codes through examination and maintain awareness of code updates and changes throughout their careers.

Examination requirements represent perhaps the most challenging aspect of state licensing for many plumbers. States typically require candidates to pass comprehensive written tests covering technical knowledge, code requirements, and safety regulations. Master plumber examinations often include additional sections on business law and project management. Some jurisdictions also require practical examinations demonstrating hands on skills.

License renewal procedures must be carefully followed to maintain valid credentials. States typically send renewal notices several months before expiration dates, but ultimate responsibility for timely renewal rests with the licensed plumber. Failing to renew on time can result in additional fees, requirements for reexamination, or complete suspension of licensing privileges.

Specialty endorsements often carry additional licensing requirements beyond standard plumbing credentials. Areas such as medical gas installation, backflow prevention, or water treatment system installation may require separate certifications or supplemental training. These specialized credentials often involve specific experience requirements and examination processes distinct from general plumbing licensure.

The complexity and variation of state licensing requirements necessitate careful research and planning by aspiring plumbers. Successful navigation of these requirements demands attention to detail, thorough record keeping, and commitment to ongoing professional development. Understanding and meeting these requirements represents a fundamental aspect of building a successful career in the plumbing industry.

Plumbing Systems Overview

The journey toward obtaining your plumbing license culminates in a series of comprehensive examinations that test your knowledge, skills, and readiness to work independently in the field. Preparing for these licensing exams requires dedication, strategic planning, and thorough understanding of both theoretical concepts and practical applications.

Success on licensing examinations begins with understanding their structure and content. Most state licensing exams consist of multiple sections covering various aspects of the plumbing trade. These typically include questions about plumbing codes and regulations, mathematics and calculations, safety procedures, materials and installation methods, troubleshooting, and system design. Master plumber examinations often incorporate additional sections on business management, employee supervision, and project planning.

Creating a comprehensive study plan represents the foundation of effective exam preparation. Begin by obtaining a current copy of your state's plumbing code and any study guides or practice materials recommended by your licensing board. Many successful candidates start their focused preparation three to six months before their scheduled examination date. This timeline allows for thorough review while maintaining a manageable pace that prevents burnout.

Practice examinations play a crucial role in preparation strategy. These mock tests help familiarize you with the exam format, time constraints, and types of questions you'll encounter. Many training programs and professional organizations offer practice exams that closely mirror the actual licensing test. Regular practice not only builds confidence but also helps identify areas where additional study may be needed.

Mathematics preparation deserves special attention during exam study. Licensing exams typically include numerous calculations related to pipe sizing, flow rates, pressure, grade, and various other plumbing system parameters. Develop proficiency with common formulas and calculations through regular practice. Pay particular attention to unit conversions, as these frequently appear in exam questions and can be a source of errors when working under pressure.

Code familiarity represents another critical aspect of exam preparation. Most licensing examinations allow candidates to use their code books during testing, but success requires knowing how to quickly locate relevant information. Create a system of tabs or notes to mark frequently referenced sections. Practice finding specific code requirements under timed conditions to build speed and efficiency in navigating the code book during the actual exam.

Diagrams and technical drawings feature prominently in many licensing examinations. Practice interpreting various types of plumbing system drawings, including isometric diagrams, floor plans, and riser diagrams. Understanding standard symbols, notation methods, and drawing conventions proves essential for correctly answering questions related to system design and troubleshooting.

Study groups can enhance exam preparation by providing opportunities for discussion, shared learning, and mutual support. Working with fellow candidates allows you to benefit from different perspectives and explanations of complex concepts. Group members can quiz each other, share study materials, and provide encouragement throughout the preparation process.

Time management during the examination requires careful preparation and practice. Most licensing exams impose strict time limits, making efficient use of available time crucial for success. Practice working through sample questions under timed conditions to develop a sense of appropriate pacing. Learn to quickly assess question difficulty and avoid spending excessive time on challenging problems at the expense of completing easier ones.

Physical preparation proves just as important as mental preparation for licensing examinations. Ensure adequate rest before the exam date and arrive at the testing location well before the scheduled start time. Familiarize yourself with the testing center's location and parking arrangements to avoid last minute stress. Bring all required materials, including your code book, calculator, and any necessary identification documents.

Practical examinations, required by some jurisdictions, demand additional preparation strategies. These hands on tests evaluate your ability to perform specific plumbing tasks according to code requirements and industry standards. Practice common installation and repair procedures under timed conditions, paying careful attention to proper sequence, tool selection, and safety protocols.

Test anxiety management strategies should form part of your preparation plan. Deep breathing exercises, positive visualization, and regular physical exercise can help reduce stress and maintain focus during study sessions and the actual examination. Remember that some nervous energy is normal and can actually enhance performance when properly channeled.

Professional review courses offer structured preparation options for licensing examinations. These programs, often available through trade schools or industry organizations, provide comprehensive review of exam content, practice questions, and test taking strategies. While not mandatory, many candidates find these courses valuable for organizing their study efforts and gaining additional insights from experienced instructors.

Documentation requirements for exam registration must be carefully reviewed and fulfilled well in advance of desired test dates. Most licensing boards require submission of work experience verification, education records, and other supporting materials before approving candidates for examination. Maintain organized records and submit required documentation early to avoid delays in scheduling your exam.

Post examination procedures vary by jurisdiction but typically include a waiting period before results become available. Use this time to maintain your knowledge and skills while avoiding excessive worry about the outcome. Many licensing boards provide detailed feedback for candidates who don't pass, allowing for focused preparation before retaking the examination.

The investment in thorough exam preparation pays dividends throughout your plumbing career. Beyond simply achieving a passing score, the knowledge and skills reinforced during preparation contribute to your professional competence and confidence. Approach the preparation process as an opportunity to solidify your understanding of the trade and establish a foundation for continued professional growth.

Basic Pipe Fitting Techniques

Every plumber needs a well-organized collection of essential hand tools to perform their work effectively and professionally. The tools you acquire at the beginning of your career will form the foundation of your daily work capabilities, and many will remain useful throughout your entire career in the plumbing trade.

The most fundamental hand tools for any beginning plumber include pipe wrenches, which come in various sizes. A typical starter set should include 14-inch and 18-inch pipe wrenches, though many experienced plumbers recommend having multiple sizes ranging from 10 inches to 24 inches. These tools are indispensable for gripping, turning, and holding pipes during installation and repair work. Quality matters significantly with pipe wrenches, as cheaper versions may slip or fail during critical operations.

Channel lock pliers represent another crucial category of hand tools. These adjustable pliers feature multiple grip positions and prove invaluable for working with various pipe sizes and fittings. Most plumbers carry at least two pairs of channel locks in different sizes to accommodate different work scenarios. The versatility of these tools makes them essential for both rough in work and finish plumbing tasks.

Basin wrenches deserve special mention as they solve the unique challenge of accessing nuts and fittings in tight spaces, particularly under sinks. This specialized tool features a long shaft with an adjustable jaw at one end, allowing plumbers to reach otherwise inaccessible areas. While you might not use a basin wrench daily, having one readily available can make certain jobs significantly easier and more professional.

A comprehensive set of screwdrivers remains essential for any plumber. Both flathead and Phillips head screwdrivers in various sizes should be part of your basic tool collection. Additionally, consider including specialty screwdrivers such as offset models for working in confined spaces. Many experienced plumbers recommend investing in screwdrivers with comfortable grips and magnetic tips for easier handling of screws.

Measurement tools form another critical category of hand tools. A good tape measure, preferably 25 feet or longer, proves essential for accurate installations and repairs. Level tools, including torpedo levels and longer models, ensure proper grade on drain lines and accurate fixture installation. A quality measuring tape should feature clear markings and a sturdy locking mechanism to prevent retraction during use.

Cutting tools represent a significant investment in your initial tool collection. Tubing cutters for both copper and plastic pipe, hacksaw, and various specialized cutters for different materials will be needed regularly. Quality cutting tools maintain sharp edges longer and produce cleaner cuts, resulting in better joint connections and more professional results.

Plumbing specific hand tools include plungers, both cup style and flanged models, which prove essential for basic drain clearing operations. Pipe reamers help remove burrs from cut pipe ends, ensuring proper fit and preventing potential flow restrictions. Thread cleaning tools maintain threaded connections and help prevent leaks in threaded joints.

Storage and organization of hand tools requires careful consideration from the beginning of your career. A sturdy tool bag or box with multiple compartments helps protect your investment and keeps tools readily accessible. Many plumbers develop personal organizational systems that allow them to quickly locate specific tools when needed, improving efficiency on job sites.

Tool maintenance practices should become part of your daily routine. Keeping tools clean, properly lubricated, and protected from moisture prevents rust and ensures reliable operation. Regular inspection of tool conditions, particularly cutting edges and moving parts, helps identify wear before it affects performance or safety.

Safety considerations influence hand tool selection and use significantly. Tools with proper insulation protect against electrical hazards when working near wiring. Ergonomic designs reduce strain during repeated use, while proper sizing ensures safe operation under various working conditions. Understanding the proper application and limitations of each tool contributes to workplace safety.

The investment in quality hand tools represents a significant expense for beginning plumbers, but attempting to save money by purchasing inferior tools often proves costly in the long run. Quality tools last longer, perform more reliably, and contribute to more professional results. Many experienced plumbers recommend purchasing the best quality you can afford for frequently used tools while choosing mid range options for less common items.

Tool selection often varies based on the specific type of plumbing work you plan to pursue. Residential service plumbers might prioritize different tools compared to new construction specialists. However, certain core tools remain essential regardless of specialization. Consulting with experienced plumbers in your intended field can help identify the most relevant tools for your situation.

As you progress in your career, your hand tool collection will naturally expand to include more specialized items. However, the basic tools acquired at the beginning of your career often remain the most frequently used. Developing proficiency with these fundamental tools builds the foundation for more advanced work and contributes to professional success in the plumbing trade.

Tool security becomes an important consideration as your collection grows. Quality tools represent a significant investment and can be attractive targets for theft. Developing good habits regarding tool security, including proper storage and tracking systems, protects your investment and ensures tools remain available when needed.

Drainage Systems

Power tools and specialized equipment represent a significant advancement in plumbing technology, enabling professionals to work more efficiently and tackle complex tasks with greater precision. While hand tools remain essential, modern plumbers rely heavily on power tools to increase productivity and handle challenging installations or repairs effectively.

The electric drill stands as perhaps the most frequently used power tool in plumbing work. A quality cordless drill with multiple batteries provides the versatility needed for various tasks, from installing anchors and hangers to drilling through studs for pipe routing. Many plumbers carry both standard drills and hammer drills, as the latter proves invaluable when working with concrete or masonry. Variable speed control and adjustable clutch settings help prevent damage to materials and ensure precise control during delicate operations.

Drain cleaning equipment forms a crucial category of powered tools in the plumbing trade. Professional grade drain cleaning machines range from small handheld units for simple clogs to large drum machines capable of clearing main sewer lines. These machines typically feature interchangeable cables and cutting heads for different pipe sizes and obstruction types. Learning to operate drain cleaning equipment safely and effectively requires significant practice and proper training to prevent damage to pipes or injury to operators.

Power pipe threading machines have revolutionized the installation of threaded pipe systems. These machines create precise threads quickly and consistently, significantly reducing the physical effort required compared to manual threading. Modern threading machines often include automatic oiling systems and adjustable speed controls. While expensive, these machines prove indispensable for commercial work or any project involving significant amounts of threaded pipe.

Pressing tools have gained widespread adoption in recent years, offering rapid and reliable pipe joining without the need for soldering or threading. These electronic or battery powered tools use specialized jaws to create permanent connections in copper, steel, or PEX piping systems. While the initial investment in pressing tools and fittings may be substantial, the time savings and reliability of connections often justify the expense for many plumbing operations.

Inspection cameras have become increasingly important in modern plumbing work. These sophisticated tools allow plumbers to visually inspect pipe interiors, identifying problems and verifying repairs without destructive investigation. Modern inspection systems often include recording capabilities and location tracking features, helping document conditions and precisely locate issues within pipe systems.

Pipe locating equipment helps identify underground piping systems and utilities before excavation work begins. These electronic tools use various technologies to detect metallic pipes, trace wire on non metallic systems, or locate specific features like septic tanks. Proficiency with locating equipment helps prevent accidental utility strikes and ensures efficient excavation operations.

Power vents and fans form another category of essential equipment, particularly for working in confined spaces or areas with potential atmospheric hazards. These tools provide necessary ventilation during soldering operations or when working in enclosed spaces. Safety considerations often dictate the use of explosion proof models in certain applications.

Hydraulic pipe benders enable precise bending of rigid pipes without kinking or damage. While manual benders work for smaller diameters, power benders handle larger pipes efficiently and produce consistent results. These machines prove particularly valuable in commercial and industrial applications where appearance and precise fit matter significantly.

Testing equipment includes various powered tools for verifying system integrity. Pressure testing pumps, vacuum pumps for AC systems, and electronic leak detectors help ensure installations meet code requirements and function properly. Modern testing equipment often includes digital readouts and data logging capabilities for documentation purposes.

Power saws of various types assist in different aspects of plumbing work. Reciprocating saws help with demolition and pipe cutting in tight spaces, while hole saws create precise openings for pipe penetrations. Battery powered tubing cutters speed up the process of cutting copper or PEX pipe while ensuring clean, square cuts.

Proper maintenance of power tools requires consistent attention to battery charging, blade or bit replacement, and lubrication of moving parts. Many plumbers establish daily maintenance routines to ensure equipment remains ready for use. Regular cleaning prevents buildup of debris that could affect tool performance or longevity.

The investment in power tools and equipment often represents one of the largest expenses for plumbing professionals or companies. Careful consideration of quality, warranty coverage, and manufacturer support helps ensure wise purchasing decisions. Many experienced plumbers recommend gradually building a power tool collection as specific needs arise rather than attempting to acquire everything at once.

Safety considerations become particularly important when using power tools. Proper training, adherence to manufacturer guidelines, and regular inspection of safety features help prevent accidents. Personal protective equipment requirements often increase when using power tools, particularly regarding eye and ear protection.

Storage and transportation of power tools requires careful planning and appropriate vehicles or storage systems. Many plumbers outfit their service vehicles with custom storage solutions to protect valuable equipment while keeping it readily accessible. Security measures help prevent theft of expensive power tools from vehicles or job sites.

As plumbing technology continues advancing, new power tools and equipment regularly enter the market. Staying informed about new developments helps plumbing professionals evaluate potential investments in equipment that could improve efficiency or capability. However, careful evaluation of cost versus benefit helps ensure wise allocation of resources when considering new technology.

Water Supply Systems

Safety equipment and protocols form the foundation of professional plumbing work, protecting both workers and clients while ensuring regulatory compliance. Every aspect of plumbing work carries inherent risks that must be carefully managed through proper equipment selection and consistent adherence to safety procedures.

Personal protective equipment (PPE) serves as the first line of defense against workplace hazards. Safety glasses or goggles protect against debris, chemicals, and flying particles during cutting, grinding, or soldering operations. Different types of eye protection suit various tasks, from basic safety glasses for general work to full face shields when working with caustic drain cleaners or sewage.

Work gloves represent another crucial component of PPE, with different types serving specific purposes. Heavy duty leather gloves protect against cuts and abrasions during general work, while chemical resistant gloves become necessary when handling solvents or cleaning agents. Heat resistant gloves protect hands during soldering or working with hot pipes, and waterproof gloves keep hands dry during extended exposure to water.

Proper footwear plays a vital role in plumbing safety. Steel toed boots protect against falling tools or materials, while non slip soles help prevent falls on wet surfaces. Waterproof boots become essential for work in flooded areas or outdoor conditions. Some situations may require additional features like electrical hazard protection or metatarsal guards.

Respiratory protection ranges from simple dust masks to sophisticated respirators depending on the working environment. When working with chemicals, dust, or in areas with potential airborne hazards, proper respiratory protection becomes crucial. Regular fit testing and maintenance of respirators ensures their effectiveness when needed.

Hard hats protect against head injuries from falling objects or low overhead clearances, particularly important in construction settings or when working in crawl spaces. Modern hard hats often incorporate additional features like attached ear protection or face shields, increasing their utility in various situations.

Hearing protection becomes essential when using power tools or working in noisy environments. Both disposable ear plugs and over ear protection have their place, with some plumbers preferring electronic hearing protection that allows normal conversation while blocking harmful noise levels.

Fall protection equipment proves vital when working at heights or in elevated positions. Safety harnesses, lanyards, and anchor points must meet specific standards and undergo regular inspection. Training in proper use and maintenance of fall protection equipment remains essential for anyone working above ground level.

Confined space entry equipment includes gas detectors, ventilation systems, and rescue equipment. Working in manholes, tanks, or crawl spaces requires careful attention to atmospheric hazards and emergency procedures. Regular calibration of gas detection equipment ensures reliable protection against invisible threats.

First aid supplies must remain readily available at all work sites. Comprehensive first aid kits should include supplies for treating common injuries like cuts, burns, and eye injuries. Many plumbing companies require workers to maintain current first aid and CPR certification.

Fire safety equipment becomes particularly important when soldering or performing hot work. Fire extinguishers must remain within easy reach, and hot work permits may be required in certain settings. Regular inspection and maintenance of fire safety equipment ensures readiness when needed.

Safety protocols begin with proper job site assessment and hazard identification. Before starting work, plumbers must evaluate potential risks and ensure appropriate safety measures are in place. This includes checking for asbestos containing materials, electrical hazards, or structural concerns that could affect worker safety.

Communication protocols help ensure all workers understand safety requirements and procedures. Clear communication about hazards, emergency procedures, and safety equipment requirements helps prevent accidents and ensures proper response if incidents occur. Many companies implement regular safety meetings and training sessions to maintain awareness.

Documentation of safety procedures and incidents helps identify trends and improve safety measures over time. Accident reports, near miss documentation, and safety inspection records provide valuable information for preventing future incidents. Regular review of safety records helps companies adjust procedures and training as needed.

Emergency response procedures must be clearly defined and understood by all workers. This includes evacuation routes, emergency contact numbers, and specific procedures for different types of incidents. Regular drills help ensure workers can respond appropriately in actual emergencies.

Vehicle safety represents another crucial aspect of plumbing work. Proper securing of tools and materials prevents hazards during transport, while regular vehicle maintenance ensures safe operation. Many companies implement specific protocols for vehicle inspection and maintenance.

Proper storage and handling of chemicals requires specific safety protocols. Safety Data Sheets must remain readily available, and proper storage facilities help prevent accidental exposure or dangerous reactions. Training in chemical handling and spill response helps prevent incidents and ensures appropriate response when needed.

Weather related safety considerations become particularly important for outdoor work. Protocols for extreme heat, cold, or electrical storms help protect workers from environmental hazards.

Proper planning and monitoring of weather conditions helps ensure worker safety in changing conditions.

Regular safety training and updates help ensure workers remain current with best practices and regulatory requirements. Many companies implement comprehensive safety programs that include both initial and ongoing training. Certification in specific safety procedures may be required for certain types of work.

Safety culture within plumbing organizations significantly impacts overall safety performance. Companies that prioritize safety through consistent enforcement of protocols, regular training, and positive reinforcement of safe practices typically experience fewer incidents. Individual commitment to safety practices helps create a workplace where everyone returns home safely each day.

Waste Disposal Systems

Reading blueprints and technical drawings represents a fundamental skill that every professional plumber must master to successfully complete installations and repairs. These documents serve as the primary means of communication between architects, engineers, contractors, and plumbers, providing essential details about the layout and specifications of plumbing systems.

Blueprints contain multiple layers of information that must be interpreted correctly to understand the full scope of a project. The basic elements include floor plans, elevation views, and section views that show different perspectives of the building and its systems. Plumbers must learn to mentally combine these different views to form a complete picture of how components interact and where potential conflicts might arise.

Standard symbols used in plumbing blueprints follow established conventions that allow professionals across the industry to interpret drawings consistently. These symbols represent fixtures, pipes, valves, and other components in a standardized way. While specific symbols might vary slightly between different firms or regions, the basic concepts remain consistent. Learning these symbols becomes second nature with experience, allowing plumbers to quickly scan drawings for relevant information.

Dimensional information on blueprints requires careful attention to scale and measurement. Most drawings include both detailed dimensions and scale references that allow measurements to be taken directly from the drawing. Understanding how to properly scale measurements helps ensure accurate material estimates and proper placement of components. Modern digital drawings often include embedded measurement tools, but the ability to work with traditional scaled drawings remains essential.

Technical specifications accompanying blueprints provide crucial details about materials, installation methods, and performance requirements. These specifications often reference building codes and industry standards that must be followed. Plumbers must be able to cross reference between drawings and specifications to ensure all requirements are met. This includes understanding how different specification sections interact and impact the overall installation.

Isometric drawings prove particularly valuable for plumbing work, as they show three dimensional relationships between components in a single view. These drawings help visualize how pipes connect and route through buildings, making them especially useful for complex installations. The ability to sketch basic isometric drawings helps plumbers communicate ideas to colleagues and clients, particularly when planning modifications to existing systems.

Working with multiple trades requires understanding how plumbing drawings relate to other building systems. Coordination with electrical, HVAC, and structural elements often becomes necessary to avoid conflicts and ensure proper installation. The ability to read and interpret drawings from other trades helps prevent costly mistakes and delays during construction.

Modern plumbing work increasingly involves digital drawings and Building Information Modeling (BIM) systems. These tools provide enhanced capabilities for visualization and coordination but require additional technical skills to utilize effectively. While traditional blueprint reading skills remain important, familiarity with digital drawing platforms becomes increasingly valuable as technology advances.

As built drawings document the actual installation of plumbing systems, often differing from original plans due to field conditions or changes during construction. Creating accurate as built documentation helps future maintenance and modifications, making it an important skill for plumbers. Understanding how to properly mark up drawings and document changes ensures valuable information is preserved for future reference.

Shop drawings provide detailed information for specific components or assemblies, often prepared by manufacturers or fabricators. These drawings require careful review to ensure compatibility with overall system design and installation requirements. The ability to interpret and verify shop drawings helps prevent issues with component fit and function.

Riser diagrams show vertical relationships between plumbing components through multiple floors of a building. These diagrams prove essential for understanding supply and drainage systems in multi story structures. Proper interpretation of riser diagrams helps ensure correct sizing and routing of vertical piping runs.

Detail drawings provide close up views of specific connections, assemblies, or installation requirements. These drawings often include specific dimensions and notes critical for proper installation. Understanding how details relate to larger system drawings helps ensure proper implementation of design requirements.

Renovation projects often involve working with incomplete or outdated drawings of existing systems. The ability to verify existing conditions and reconcile differences between drawings and reality becomes crucial. Experience in reading older drawings and documenting existing conditions helps plumbers work effectively in renovation settings.

Notes and schedules on drawings provide important information about fixtures, equipment, and installation requirements. These elements often contain crucial details not shown graphically in the drawings. Careful attention to notes and schedules helps ensure all requirements are identified and addressed during installation.

Successful blueprint reading requires developing a systematic approach to drawing review and interpretation. Starting with an overview of the complete drawing set before focusing on specific areas helps understand context and relationships between different components. Regular practice and exposure to various types of drawings builds proficiency over time.

Gas Piping

Understanding plumbing systems forms the foundation of every plumber's knowledge base. A plumbing system represents an intricate network of pipes, fixtures, and appliances that work together to deliver clean water, remove waste, and maintain proper pressure throughout a building. Mastering these systems requires comprehensive knowledge of how each component functions both independently and as part of the larger whole.

The basic concept of a plumbing system revolves around two primary networks: the water supply system and the drainage system. These networks operate under different principles, with supply lines maintaining pressure to deliver water where needed, while drainage relies on gravity and proper venting to remove waste effectively. Understanding the relationship between these systems helps plumbers diagnose problems and design efficient solutions.

Water pressure plays a crucial role in plumbing system functionality. Too much pressure can damage pipes and fixtures, while insufficient pressure leads to poor performance. Plumbers must understand how pressure varies throughout a system and how different components affect pressure levels. This knowledge helps in proper sizing of pipes and selection of appropriate pressure regulation devices.

Temperature control represents another vital aspect of plumbing systems. Hot water delivery requires careful consideration of heat loss, circulation, and safety measures to prevent scalding. Understanding how water heaters interact with distribution systems helps ensure consistent and safe hot water delivery throughout a building. This includes knowledge of recirculation systems, mixing valves, and insulation requirements.

Venting systems maintain proper pressure balance in drainage pipes and prevent siphoning of trap seals. The relationship between vents and drains follows specific rules regarding size, distance, and configuration.

Understanding these requirements helps plumbers design effective venting solutions that ensure proper drainage while protecting against sewer gas infiltration.

Cross connection control protects potable water supplies from contamination. Plumbers must understand various backflow prevention methods and where they should be applied. This includes knowledge of air gaps, vacuum breakers, and backflow preventers, as well as regular testing and maintenance requirements for these devices.

Fixture units help determine proper pipe sizing based on anticipated water usage. Understanding how to calculate fixture units and apply them to sizing tables ensures adequate flow without oversizing systems unnecessarily. This knowledge proves particularly important in commercial applications where multiple fixtures operate simultaneously.

Storm drainage systems manage rainwater and prevent flooding around buildings. These systems often interact with sanitary drainage but must remain separate to prevent overwhelming treatment facilities. Understanding proper sizing and routing of storm drainage helps protect buildings from water damage while complying with local regulations.

Water treatment systems improve water quality for specific applications. From simple filtration to complex purification systems, plumbers must understand various treatment methods and their appropriate applications. This includes knowledge of water testing, filter selection, and maintenance requirements for different treatment systems.

Pump systems overcome elevation differences and pressure limitations in plumbing systems. Understanding pump selection, installation, and troubleshooting helps ensure reliable water delivery in challenging situations. This includes knowledge of different pump types, control systems, and maintenance requirements.

Gas piping systems often fall under plumbing responsibilities, requiring additional knowledge of safety requirements and installation methods. Understanding gas system design, pressure testing, and ventilation requirements helps ensure safe and efficient fuel delivery. This includes knowledge of different fuel types and their specific installation requirements.

Building automation systems increasingly integrate with plumbing components to improve efficiency and monitoring capabilities. Understanding how sensors, controllers, and automated valves interact helps plumbers work effectively with modern building systems. This includes knowledge of basic control principles and troubleshooting methods for automated components.

Piping materials selection requires understanding various factors including pressure ratings, temperature limitations, and chemical compatibility. Knowledge of different materials' strengths and weaknesses helps ensure appropriate selection for specific applications. This includes understanding how different materials handle expansion, support requirements, and joining methods.

System testing and commissioning verify proper operation before putting new installations into service. Understanding various testing methods and acceptance criteria helps ensure systems meet design requirements and operate safely. This includes knowledge of pressure testing, flow testing, and documentation requirements.

Maintenance considerations should influence system design and component selection. Understanding common maintenance requirements helps create systems that remain serviceable throughout their lifetime. This includes providing appropriate access points and selecting components with proven reliability records.

Emergency shutoff capabilities protect buildings from damage during system failures. Understanding proper placement and selection of shutoff valves helps ensure quick response to emergencies. This includes knowledge of valve types, access requirements, and identification methods.

Through comprehensive understanding of these various aspects, plumbers can effectively design, install, and maintain plumbing systems that provide reliable service while protecting public health and safety. This knowledge base continues to evolve as new technologies and methods emerge, requiring ongoing education and adaptation to changing industry standards.

Plumbing Fixtures and Appliances

Water supply systems form one of the most critical components of modern plumbing infrastructure, delivering clean, potable water to homes and businesses while maintaining appropriate pressure and quality standards throughout the distribution network. These systems begin at the municipal water main or private well and extend throughout buildings through an intricate network of pipes, valves, and fixtures designed to provide reliable water service.

The journey of water through a supply system starts with the main connection, typically featuring a meter to track usage and a main shutoff valve. This connection point requires careful consideration of local codes and pressure requirements, as incoming pressure often needs regulation to protect internal plumbing components. Understanding pressure regulators and their proper installation becomes essential for maintaining consistent, safe water pressure throughout the building.

Distribution piping forms the backbone of the water supply system, branching from main lines to serve various fixtures and appliances. Pipe sizing plays a crucial role in system performance, requiring careful calculation of fixture units and anticipated demand. Undersized pipes can result in pressure loss and poor performance, while oversized pipes waste materials and can lead to stagnation issues. Plumbers must master the art of proper pipe sizing to create efficient, cost effective systems.

Hot water distribution presents unique challenges within the supply system. Water heaters, whether tank type or tankless, must be properly sized and positioned to serve their intended loads effectively. Recirculation systems often prove necessary in larger buildings to provide quick hot water access while minimizing water waste. These systems require careful balancing of pump sizing, pipe insulation, and control strategies to operate efficiently.

Material selection for water supply systems demands thorough understanding of various options including copper, PEX, CPVC, and other approved materials. Each material offers distinct advantages and limitations regarding cost, durability, installation methods, and chemical compatibility. Plumbers must consider factors such as water chemistry, pressure requirements, and temperature ranges when selecting appropriate materials for specific applications.

Fixture connections represent the final link in water supply systems, requiring proper installation techniques to prevent leaks and ensure reliable operation. Understanding different connection methods, from compression fittings to soldered joints, helps plumbers create secure, long lasting installations. This includes knowledge of proper support methods, expansion allowances, and isolation valves for servicability.

Water quality protection plays a vital role in supply system design and maintenance. Backflow prevention devices must be installed where required to protect potable water from contamination. Regular testing and maintenance of these devices ensures continued protection of the water supply. Plumbers must understand various backflow prevention methods and their appropriate applications.

Pressure maintenance within supply systems requires careful attention to elevation changes and friction losses. Booster pumps may become necessary in tall buildings or areas with low municipal pressure. Understanding pump selection, installation requirements, and control strategies helps ensure reliable water delivery throughout the system. This includes considerations for emergency power and redundancy in critical applications.

Water treatment systems often integrate with supply systems to address specific quality issues. From basic filtration to complex purification systems, plumbers must understand various treatment methods and their proper installation. This includes consideration of maintenance access, filter replacement requirements, and appropriate bypass provisions for servicing.

System maintenance and troubleshooting form essential aspects of water supply work. Understanding common problems and their solutions helps plumbers quickly diagnose and repair issues. This includes knowledge of pressure testing methods, leak detection techniques, and water quality testing procedures. Regular maintenance helps prevent costly failures and extends system life.

Winterization considerations become crucial in cold climates, requiring proper installation of freeze protection measures. This includes appropriate pipe insulation, heat trace systems, and drainage provisions for seasonal systems. Understanding freeze protection methods helps prevent costly damage during cold weather periods.

Smart technology increasingly integrates with water supply systems, offering enhanced monitoring and control capabilities. Flow sensors, leak detection systems, and automated shutoff valves provide additional protection and convenience. Plumbers must understand how these technologies integrate with traditional plumbing components and building automation systems.

Water conservation measures continue gaining importance in supply system design. Low flow fixtures, pressure reduction strategies, and water reuse systems help minimize consumption while maintaining functionality. Understanding various conservation methods helps plumbers create systems that meet both performance and efficiency goals.

Through comprehensive understanding of water supply systems, plumbers can design and install reliable networks that provide safe, efficient water delivery while protecting valuable resources. This knowledge continues expanding as new technologies and methods emerge, requiring ongoing education and adaptation to changing industry standards.

Troubleshooting Common Plumbing Problems

Drainage systems represent a critical component of any plumbing installation, serving the essential function of removing wastewater and other liquids from buildings safely and efficiently. These systems rely on gravity and careful engineering to transport waste through a complex network of pipes, fittings, and other components that must work together seamlessly to prevent backups, leaks, and sanitation issues.

The foundation of any drainage system begins with proper slope, typically requiring a minimum fall of one quarter inch per foot for most applications. This careful grading ensures waste flows smoothly through the system while maintaining adequate velocity to prevent buildup and blockages. Understanding proper slope calculations and installation techniques becomes essential for creating effective drainage networks that will perform reliably for decades.

Pipe sizing in drainage systems follows different principles than supply systems, requiring careful consideration of fixture units and anticipated peak loads. Unlike pressurized supply lines, drain lines must be sized to handle intermittent heavy flows while maintaining adequate venting. The relationship between pipe diameter, slope, and flow capacity requires thorough understanding to prevent both oversizing and undersizing issues that could compromise system performance.

Branch lines connecting individual fixtures to main drain lines require particular attention to detail. Each fixture type has specific requirements for trap size, arm length, and venting arrangements. Understanding these requirements helps prevent common issues like slow draining fixtures, gurgling sounds, and siphoned traps that could allow sewer gases into living spaces.

Main drain lines serve as the primary collection points for multiple fixture branches, requiring careful planning of connections and cleanout locations. Access for maintenance becomes crucial, as even well designed systems eventually require cleaning or inspection. Strategic placement of cleanouts allows for efficient servicing while maintaining system integrity.

Building drain systems connect interior plumbing to exterior sewer or septic connections, often requiring coordination with other trades and careful attention to elevation requirements. Understanding local codes regarding minimum burial depths, support requirements, and materials becomes essential for creating compliant installations that will pass inspection.

Floor drains and area drains present unique challenges in both residential and commercial applications. Proper placement and sizing of these components helps prevent flooding while maintaining sanitary conditions. Understanding slope requirements around floor drains and appropriate grate selection for various applications ensures effective drainage in wet areas.

Commercial kitchen drainage requires specialized knowledge of grease interceptors and proper sizing for food service applications. Understanding grease trap maintenance requirements and local regulations regarding fats, oils, and grease helps create systems that protect both building plumbing and municipal infrastructure from costly damage.

Storm drainage systems often integrate with sanitary drainage, requiring careful attention to local codes regarding combined versus separate systems. Roof drains, area drains, and collection systems must handle peak loads during heavy rainfall while preventing backup into buildings. Understanding rainfall intensity data and proper sizing methods helps create reliable storm drainage installations.

Indirect waste requirements protect potable water systems from contamination while allowing proper drainage from specific fixtures and equipment. Understanding air gap requirements and proper receptor sizing helps create safe, code compliant installations for applications like commercial dishwashers and food preparation equipment.

Special waste systems handle materials that require separate treatment or disposal methods. Laboratory waste, chemical waste, and other specialized applications often require specific materials and installation methods. Understanding these requirements helps create appropriate systems for various industrial and institutional applications.

Testing drainage systems requires thorough knowledge of appropriate methods and local requirements. Whether using water tests, air tests, or smoke testing, proper procedures help ensure system integrity before walls and floors are closed. Understanding various testing methods and their applications helps verify installations will perform as intended.

Maintenance considerations must factor into drainage system design, including appropriate access for cleaning and inspection. Understanding common problem areas and maintenance requirements helps create systems that can be effectively serviced throughout their life cycle. This includes consideration for future modifications or expansions that might become necessary.

Troubleshooting drainage issues requires systematic approach and thorough understanding of system components. From simple clogs to complex venting problems, knowing common failure points and their solutions helps quickly resolve issues. This includes familiarity with various diagnostic tools and techniques for identifying problems efficiently.

Modern drainage systems increasingly incorporate monitoring and maintenance features. From simple cleanout locations to complex monitoring systems that detect potential issues before they become problems, technology continues expanding options for system management. Understanding these advances helps create more reliable and maintainable installations.

Through comprehensive understanding of drainage system principles and requirements, plumbers can create effective networks that reliably serve their intended purposes while protecting public health and safety. This knowledge base continues expanding as new technologies and methods emerge, requiring ongoing education and adaptation to changing industry standards.

Basic Plumbing Repairs

Venting systems serve as the lungs of a building's plumbing network, playing a vital role in maintaining proper drainage function and protecting public health. Without adequate venting, even the best designed drainage systems can fail, leading to slow drains, gurgling noises, and potentially dangerous sewer gas infiltration into living spaces.

The primary purpose of a plumbing vent system is to equalize air pressure within drainage pipes, allowing waste to flow freely while preventing trap seal loss. As water flows through drain pipes, it creates pressure fluctuations that must be balanced through proper venting. This pressure equalization protects trap seals that prevent sewer gases from entering buildings while ensuring efficient drainage flow.

Stack vents form the backbone of most venting systems, extending vertically through buildings to the atmosphere. These main vent stacks typically connect to the building drain near its base and continue undiminished in size through the roof. Understanding proper sizing and installation requirements for stack vents becomes crucial, as these components must handle the cumulative venting needs of multiple fixtures while resisting weather exposure at their termination points.

Branch vents serve individual fixtures or small groups of fixtures, connecting them to the main stack vent system. These smaller vent lines must be carefully sized and configured to provide adequate air flow while preventing potential blockage from condensation or debris. Understanding maximum length limitations and proper slope requirements helps ensure reliable long term performance of branch vent systems.

Wet venting represents an efficient method of combining drain and vent functions in certain applications, reducing the total amount of piping required. However, wet venting must follow specific rules regarding fixture types, pipe sizing, and arrangement to maintain proper function. Understanding these requirements helps create efficient installations that meet code requirements while minimizing materials and labor.

Circuit venting and loop venting provide solutions for multiple fixtures on the same drain line, particularly in commercial applications with battery style fixture arrangements. These specialized venting methods require careful attention to sizing and configuration requirements to ensure adequate air flow for all connected fixtures. Understanding appropriate applications for different venting methods helps create efficient, code compliant installations.

Relief vents become necessary in certain situations where standard venting arrangements cannot provide adequate air flow. Understanding when and where relief vents are required helps prevent potential system failures while ensuring code compliance. This includes knowledge of maximum developed length limitations and proper connection methods.

Air admittance valves offer alternative venting solutions in situations where conventional through roof venting proves impractical. While these devices can provide effective venting in appropriate applications, understanding their limitations and installation requirements becomes crucial. This includes knowledge of proper sizing, accessibility requirements, and situations where their use is prohibited.

Island fixture venting presents unique challenges, particularly in kitchen installations where conventional overhead venting may not be possible. Understanding various approaches to island venting, including loop vents and air admittance valves, helps create functional solutions that maintain proper drainage while meeting aesthetic requirements.

Frost closure in vent systems can create serious problems in cold climates, requiring careful attention to insulation and routing requirements. Understanding minimum size requirements for vent extensions through roofs and proper protection methods helps prevent winter related failures that could compromise entire plumbing systems.

Special venting requirements apply to specific fixtures and situations, such as sump pumps, ejector systems, and grease interceptors. Understanding these specialized requirements helps create appropriate venting solutions that ensure reliable operation while protecting public health and safety.

Common venting problems often stem from improper sizing, excessive length, or inadequate connections. Understanding typical failure points and their solutions helps both in creating new installations and troubleshooting existing systems. This includes familiarity with various testing methods to verify proper vent system function.

Modern plumbing systems increasingly incorporate innovative venting solutions that can reduce material requirements while maintaining proper function. Understanding these emerging technologies and their appropriate applications helps create more efficient installations while ensuring code compliance and system reliability.

The interaction between venting and drainage systems requires comprehensive understanding of both components to create effective plumbing installations. As building designs become more complex and water conservation measures affect traditional flow patterns, proper venting becomes increasingly crucial for system performance.

Through thorough understanding of venting principles and requirements, plumbers can create effective systems that ensure reliable drainage function while protecting public health and safety. This knowledge continues expanding as new technologies and methods emerge, requiring ongoing education and adaptation to changing industry standards.

Emergency Plumbing Repairs

Installing fixtures and appliances represents one of the most visible and satisfying aspects of plumbing work, as it transforms rough plumbing into functional elements that clients use daily. Success in this area requires not only technical knowledge but also attention to detail and a thorough understanding of manufacturer specifications and local codes.

The process begins with careful planning and preparation of the installation site. Before any fixture installation, plumbers must verify that rough in dimensions match the specifications for the particular fixture being installed. This includes checking center lines, height requirements, and ensuring adequate clearances for both installation and future maintenance. Even small discrepancies at this stage can lead to significant problems later.

Water closet installation serves as a prime example of the precision required in fixture work. The process starts with inspecting the closet flange for proper positioning and securing it if necessary. Setting a new wax ring requires careful alignment to prevent future leaks, while positioning the toilet demands attention to level and proper compression of the seal. Understanding various mounting systems, including standard floor bolts and modern speed connect systems, helps ensure secure installation that will stand up to years of use.

Lavatory installations present their own unique challenges, particularly when dealing with various mounting styles. Pedestal sinks require careful coordination of drain and supply rough ins, while wall hung models demand proper support blocking and careful attention to mounting height requirements. Understanding proper installation sequences helps prevent common issues such as drain alignment problems or inadequate support.

Bathtub and shower installations often represent some of the most complex fixture work, requiring coordination with multiple trades and careful attention to waterproofing details. Whether installing prefabricated units or custom tile assemblies, proper support and leveling become crucial for long term performance. Understanding various waste and overflow assemblies and their installation requirements helps prevent future leakage issues.

Kitchen sink installations demand attention to both functional and aesthetic considerations. Understanding various mounting styles, including top mount, undermount, and farmhouse configurations, helps ensure proper installation that meets client expectations. Coordination with countertop fabricators becomes essential, particularly for undermount installations where timing and precise measurements prove critical.

Dishwasher installation requires understanding both plumbing and electrical requirements, as well as proper integration with cabinetry and countertops. Proper installation of air gaps or high loop arrangements helps prevent potential contamination of water supplies, while attention to leveling and securing prevents future operational issues.

Water heater installations combine multiple skills, from basic plumbing connections to possible gas or electrical work depending on the unit type. Understanding various safety requirements, including temperature and pressure relief valve installation, proper venting for gas units, and seismic restraint requirements in applicable areas, helps create safe and reliable installations.

Garbage disposal installation requires familiarity with both plumbing and electrical connections, as well as proper mounting techniques. Understanding various types of mounting systems and their installation requirements helps ensure secure attachment and proper alignment with sink drains. Knowledge of local codes regarding disposal use and installation becomes particularly important in areas with restricted sewer systems.

Commercial fixture installation often involves specialized equipment and mounting systems, particularly in public restrooms and institutional settings. Understanding requirements for accessibility compliance, vandal resistance, and high use applications helps create installations that meet both functional and durability requirements.

Proper fixture installation also requires understanding various connection methods for water supplies and drain lines. Knowledge of different supply stop types, flexible connector requirements, and proper support methods helps prevent future maintenance issues. Understanding trap requirements and proper installation techniques ensures reliable drainage while maintaining necessary trap seals.

The increasing popularity of smart fixtures and touchless technology adds another layer of complexity to modern installations. Understanding electronic components, battery systems, and proper sensor positioning helps ensure reliable operation of these advanced fixtures. Knowledge of troubleshooting procedures for electronic systems becomes increasingly important as these fixtures become more common.

Water conservation requirements increasingly affect fixture selection and installation, particularly in areas with severe water restrictions. Understanding flow rate requirements and various water saving technologies helps create installations that meet both regulatory requirements and user expectations. This includes familiarity with various flow reducers, aerators, and pressure compensating devices.

Quality fixture installation also requires attention to finishing details such as proper caulking and sealing. Understanding various sealant types and their appropriate applications helps prevent water damage while creating aesthetically pleasing installations. Knowledge of proper cleaning and protection methods helps ensure fixtures maintain their appearance through project completion.

Success in fixture installation ultimately comes from combining technical knowledge with practical experience and attention to detail.

Understanding not just how fixtures go together but why specific methods and requirements exist helps create installations that provide long term reliability while meeting both code requirements and client expectations.

Pipe Materials and Their Uses

This chapter focuses on the various pipe materials used in modern plumbing systems and their specific applications. Understanding pipe materials represents a crucial foundation of plumbing work, as selecting the right material for each application directly impacts system performance, longevity, and code compliance.

Copper piping remains one of the most widely used materials in residential and commercial plumbing, particularly for water supply lines. Its natural antimicrobial properties, durability, and reliability have made it a standard in the industry for decades. Type K copper, with its thicker walls, serves well for underground applications, while Type L sees common use in interior water lines. Type M, being thinner, typically finds use in residential applications where codes permit. Copper's main advantages include its long lifespan, resistance to corrosion, and ability to handle both hot and cold applications. However, its increasing cost and vulnerability to acidic water conditions require careful consideration during material selection.

PEX (cross linked polyethylene) has revolutionized residential plumbing in recent decades. Its flexibility, ease of installation, and resistance to freezing make it increasingly popular for water supply systems. The material's ability to expand and contract helps prevent burst pipes in freezing conditions, while its smooth interior walls resist mineral buildup. Different color coding (red for hot, blue for cold) simplifies installation and future identification. PEX's main limitations include UV sensitivity and the need for special tools and fittings.

PVC (polyvinyl chloride) dominates drainage applications, particularly in residential settings. Schedule 40 PVC serves well for most drain, waste, and vent applications above ground, while Schedule 80 provides extra thickness for more demanding situations. PVC's lightweight nature, chemical resistance, and ease of installation make it ideal for many applications. However, its temperature limitations restrict use for hot water lines, and some jurisdictions limit its use in certain applications.

CPVC (chlorinated polyvinyl chloride) offers higher temperature resistance than standard PVC, making it suitable for hot and cold water distribution. Its chemical resistance and ease of installation make it popular in both residential and commercial applications. However, its higher cost compared to standard PVC and potential for brittleness over time require consideration during system design.

Cast iron pipe, though less common in new construction, remains important in commercial and industrial applications where noise reduction or fire ratings are crucial. Its excellent sound dampening properties make it ideal for multi story buildings where drainage noise could be problematic. Modern installation methods, including no hub couplings, have simplified working with this traditional material, though its weight and cost often limit its use to specific applications.

ABS (acrylonitrile butadiene styrene) pipe serves as an alternative to PVC in some drainage applications, particularly in residential construction. Its single wall black construction makes it easily identifiable, while its impact resistance and ease of installation make it popular in some regions. However, regional code restrictions and UV sensitivity can limit its applications.

Stainless steel pipe finds extensive use in specialized applications, particularly in food processing facilities, breweries, and medical installations where absolute cleanliness is essential. Its corrosion resistance and ability to handle high temperatures make it ideal for these demanding applications, though its high cost typically limits use to specific situations where its unique properties justify the expense.

Galvanized steel pipe, once common for water supply lines, now sees limited use primarily in gas lines and some industrial applications. Understanding its limitations becomes particularly important when working on older systems, as corrosion issues often necessitate replacement with modern materials.

HDPE (high density polyethylene) pipe has gained popularity in outdoor and underground applications, particularly for water service lines and drainage systems. Its flexibility, chemical resistance, and ability to handle ground movement make it ideal for these applications. However, special fusion welding equipment requirements and temperature limitations restrict its use in some situations.

Understanding proper transitions between different pipe materials proves crucial for successful installations. Knowledge of various adapter types, dielectric unions for dissimilar metals, and proper support requirements helps prevent future problems. Additionally, awareness of local code requirements regarding acceptable materials and applications ensures compliant installations.

Material selection also requires consideration of environmental factors, including soil conditions for underground installations, UV exposure for exterior applications, and chemical exposure in industrial settings. Understanding how different materials react to these conditions helps ensure appropriate material selection for each application.

Cost considerations play an important role in material selection, requiring balance between initial installation costs and long term durability. Understanding life cycle costs, including maintenance requirements and replacement intervals, helps inform material choices that provide the best value for specific applications.

The ongoing development of new pipe materials and installation methods requires plumbers to stay current with industry advances. Understanding both the advantages and limitations of new materials helps ensure appropriate application while maintaining necessary safety and reliability standards.

Success in the plumbing trade requires not just knowledge of various pipe materials but understanding their proper application, installation requirements, and limitations. This comprehensive understanding helps create plumbing systems that provide reliable service while meeting both current needs and future requirements.

Joining Pipes

This chapter focuses on joining methods and techniques used in plumbing systems, a critical skill set that every plumber must master to create reliable and code compliant installations. The ability to properly join pipes and fittings represents one of the most fundamental aspects of plumbing work, as system integrity depends entirely on the quality of these connections.

Soldering, often called sweating, remains one of the most important joining methods for copper piping systems. This process requires careful preparation, including proper cleaning of both pipe and fitting surfaces, application of appropriate flux, and careful heating to achieve the correct temperature for solder flow. Understanding the importance of capillary action in creating strong joints helps ensure reliable connections. Proper soldering technique involves methodically heating the fitting and pipe while avoiding overheating that could damage the copper or nearby materials. The selection of appropriate solder, particularly lead free varieties for potable water systems, proves crucial for both safety and code compliance.

Threading represents another traditional joining method that remains important, particularly for steel pipe installations. Creating proper threads requires careful attention to cutting depth, thread taper, and overall thread quality. Understanding proper application of pipe joint compounds or tape ensures leak free connections while maintaining system integrity. The importance of proper pipe support and alignment during threading operations cannot be overstated, as misalignment can lead to joint failure.

Modern press fitting systems have revolutionized many aspects of plumbing installation, particularly in copper and stainless steel systems. These systems utilize specialized tools to create permanent mechanical connections without the need for heat or threading. Understanding proper insertion depth, tool maintenance, and manufacturer specific requirements ensures reliable connections. While the initial investment in tools can be significant, the time savings and reliability of properly executed press connections often justify the expense.

PVC and CPVC systems typically utilize solvent welding for joining, a process that requires understanding of proper cleaning, primer application where required, and cement selection. Temperature and humidity conditions can significantly affect joint quality, making awareness of environmental conditions crucial. Proper technique includes checking insertion depth, ensuring even cement application, and maintaining proper alignment during the initial setting period. Understanding cure times for different sizes and conditions helps prevent premature system pressurization.

PEX systems employ several joining methods, including crimp rings, clamp rings, and expansion fittings. Each system requires specific tools and techniques, making understanding manufacturer requirements essential. Proper calibration of tools and regular verification of joint quality help ensure system reliability. The importance of proper support and consideration of thermal expansion characteristics cannot be overlooked when installing PEX systems.

Mechanical joints, including no hub couplings for cast iron and various transition fittings, require understanding proper torque requirements and installation sequences. Awareness of proper gasket installation and the importance of clean, undamaged sealing surfaces helps ensure leak free connections. Understanding the limitations of different coupling systems and their appropriate applications prevents future problems.

Fusion welding, particularly for HDPE pipe, requires specialized equipment and careful attention to proper procedures. Understanding proper heating times, fusion pressures, and cooling requirements ensures strong, reliable joints. The importance of proper cleaning and alignment during the fusion process cannot be overstated, as errors during fusion welding typically cannot be corrected without cutting out and replacing the affected section.

Grooved mechanical joints, common in commercial and industrial applications, require understanding proper pipe preparation, gasket selection, and coupling installation. Knowledge of torque requirements and proper lubrication ensures reliable connections. Understanding the advantages and limitations of rigid versus flexible couplings helps ensure appropriate application.

Special consideration must be given to joining dissimilar materials, particularly in situations involving different metals where galvanic corrosion could occur. Understanding proper use of dielectric unions and appropriate transition fittings helps prevent future problems. Awareness of thermal expansion characteristics of different materials ensures proper installation of expansion joints or loops where required.

Quality control procedures play a crucial role in joint installation, including proper inspection of completed joints and appropriate testing methods. Understanding common failure modes and their causes helps prevent installation problems. Regular calibration of tools and verification of proper function ensures consistent joint quality.

Safety considerations during joining operations include proper ventilation when working with solvent cements, appropriate fire protection during soldering operations, and proper use of personal protective equipment. Understanding proper handling of tools and materials helps prevent injuries while ensuring quality installations.

The ongoing development of new joining methods and materials requires continuous learning and adaptation of techniques. Understanding both traditional and modern joining methods provides the flexibility to work with various systems while maintaining high quality standards. Success in the plumbing trade requires not just knowledge of joining methods but the skill to execute them properly under various field conditions.

Advanced Pipe Fitting

This chapter focuses on troubleshooting common plumbing problems, a vital skill that separates experienced plumbers from novices. The ability to quickly and accurately diagnose issues saves time, reduces customer frustration, and builds a plumber's reputation for competence and reliability.

Low water pressure represents one of the most frequent complaints encountered in residential plumbing. A systematic approach to diagnosis begins with determining whether the issue affects all fixtures or just specific ones. Whole house pressure problems often stem from main valve issues, pressure reducer malfunctions, or municipal supply problems. Individual fixture problems typically relate to clogged aerators, damaged cartridges, or localized pipe restrictions. Understanding the building's plumbing layout and pressure zones helps narrow down potential causes quickly.

Drain blockages require careful analysis to determine the most effective clearing method. Simple sink clogs might respond to plunging or basic cable work, while main line stoppages often demand more powerful equipment and different approaches. Knowledge of common problem areas, such as kitchen lines prone to grease buildup or bathroom drains affected by hair accumulation, helps guide initial diagnostic efforts. Understanding drain system architecture, including the location of cleanouts and vents, proves crucial for efficient troubleshooting.

Water heater problems present unique challenges due to the interaction of multiple systems. Issues might stem from fuel supply, thermostat malfunction, sediment buildup, or deteriorated components. Understanding the relationship between symptoms and potential causes helps direct diagnostic efforts efficiently. For example, inadequate hot water might indicate a failed heating element, while rusty water often suggests tank corrosion. The ability to interpret these signs correctly leads to faster, more accurate repairs.

Toilet malfunctions encompass a range of issues from simple flapper problems to more complex siphon jet blockages. Understanding the mechanical operation of different toilet designs helps identify likely failure points. Problems like phantom flushes, weak flushing, or continuous running each suggest specific component failures. The ability to quickly identify the actual cause rather than simply replacing parts at random marks the professional approach to toilet repair.

Leaking pipes require careful investigation to locate the source accurately. Surface water might travel significant distances from the actual leak point, making visual inspection misleading. Understanding common failure points, such as joints near anchoring points or areas subject to mechanical stress, helps focus the search. Modern leak detection equipment, including acoustic sensors and thermal imaging, provides additional tools for difficult cases.

Sewer line problems demand particular attention due to their potential severity and impact. Understanding the signs of main line issues, such as multiple drain backups or gurgling toilets, allows early intervention before major failures occur. Knowledge of common causes, including root intrusion, pipe collapse, or offset joints, helps guide inspection and repair strategies. Familiarity with various diagnostic tools, from simple cable machines to sophisticated camera systems, enables accurate problem identification.

Fixture problems require understanding both mechanical operation and common wear patterns. Faucet repairs, for instance, might involve cartridge replacement, seal renewal, or more extensive work depending on the specific design and symptoms. Knowledge of different manufacturers' designs and common failure points helps speed diagnosis and repair. Understanding parts interchangeability and upgrade options provides additional solution possibilities.

Water hammer and other noise issues often prove challenging to diagnose due to sound transmission through building structures. Understanding the relationship between system design, pressure conditions, and noise generation helps identify likely causes. Knowledge of solutions, from simple air chamber maintenance to installation of specialized arrestors, enables effective problem resolution.

Gas system problems require particular attention due to safety implications. Understanding the relationship between pressure, volume, and appliance operation helps diagnose supply issues. Knowledge of common failure points, including regulator problems, appliance malfunctions, or pipe restrictions, guides safe and effective troubleshooting. The ability to properly test systems and identify potential hazards proves crucial for gas work.

Frozen pipe prevention and repair requires understanding both immediate solutions and long term prevention strategies. Knowledge of typical freeze points, pipe protection methods, and proper thawing techniques helps address immediate problems while preventing future occurrences. Understanding the relationship between building design, insulation, and freeze risk enables development of effective prevention strategies.

Cross connection and backflow issues demand careful attention due to their potential health implications. Understanding system design requirements, common failure points, and proper testing procedures ensures safe water supply maintenance. Knowledge of various backflow prevention devices and their appropriate applications helps address problems effectively while ensuring code compliance.

Successful troubleshooting requires not just technical knowledge but also the ability to gather accurate information from customers and interpret it correctly. Understanding how to ask effective questions, observe relevant symptoms, and correlate various pieces of information leads to faster, more accurate diagnosis. The ability to explain problems and solutions clearly to customers while maintaining professional credibility marks the successful plumbing technician.

Introduction to Blueprints and Schematics

Emergency response and repair work represents one of the most challenging yet rewarding aspects of the plumbing profession. When emergencies strike, plumbers must combine technical expertise with quick thinking and calm decision making to address potentially devastating situations. This chapter explores the essential skills and knowledge needed to handle plumbing emergencies effectively.

Water emergencies typically demand immediate attention due to their potential for property damage. Burst pipes, especially during freezing conditions, can release hundreds of gallons of water within minutes. The first priority in such situations involves locating and shutting off the appropriate water supply valve. Understanding building water systems and valve locations proves crucial for quick response. Professional plumbers develop mental maps of typical plumbing layouts, enabling them to quickly identify likely shutoff points even in unfamiliar buildings.

Flooding scenarios require rapid assessment and strategic planning. Beyond immediate water shutoff, plumbers must evaluate structural impacts, electrical hazards, and potential contamination issues. Knowledge of water extraction methods, drying techniques, and sanitization procedures helps minimize property damage and health risks. Understanding when to coordinate with other professionals, such as electricians or restoration specialists, ensures comprehensive emergency response.

Sewer backups create particularly challenging emergency situations. These events often occur during storms or peak usage periods, requiring response in difficult conditions. Understanding municipal sewer systems, building plumbing architecture, and backup causes helps guide immediate response efforts. Knowledge of various clearing methods, from basic cable machines to high pressure jetting systems, enables selection of the most effective approach for each situation.

Gas leaks demand especially careful emergency response due to explosion and health risks. Plumbers must understand proper gas detection methods, shutdown procedures, and ventilation requirements. Knowledge of gas system components, common failure points, and repair techniques enables safe and effective emergency response. Understanding when to involve gas utility companies or other emergency services proves crucial for public safety.

Hot water system failures, particularly in commercial settings, often require emergency response. Understanding various water heater types, common failure modes, and temporary bypass options helps maintain essential services while permanent repairs proceed. Knowledge of local codes regarding temporary solutions ensures compliance while addressing immediate needs.

Commercial kitchen emergencies present unique challenges due to health code requirements and business interruption costs. Understanding grease waste systems, commercial fixtures, and health department regulations helps guide emergency response efforts. Knowledge of temporary solutions that maintain operational capability while ensuring code compliance proves valuable in these situations.

Medical facility plumbing emergencies require particular attention due to patient care implications. Understanding medical gas systems, sterilization requirements, and infection control protocols guides emergency response in these sensitive environments. Knowledge of backup systems and temporary solutions helps maintain essential services during repairs.

Apartment building emergencies often involve multiple affected units and complex access issues. Understanding building systems, resident rights, and property management protocols helps coordinate effective emergency response. Knowledge of temporary solutions and repair prioritization helps manage complex situations involving multiple residents.

Weather related emergencies, such as frozen pipes or storm damage, often occur in clusters, requiring efficient resource management. Understanding prevention techniques, temporary protection methods, and repair prioritization helps address multiple emergencies effectively. Knowledge of material availability and alternate suppliers proves valuable during widespread events.

Emergency response requires more than technical skills. The ability to communicate clearly with distressed customers, coordinate with other emergency services, and manage multiple priorities simultaneously proves essential. Understanding insurance procedures, documentation requirements, and liability issues helps protect both customers and plumbing professionals during emergency situations.

Equipment preparation plays a crucial role in emergency response capability. Maintaining fully stocked emergency response vehicles, including specialized tools and commonly needed materials, enables quick effective response. Understanding seasonal emergency patterns helps guide inventory management and equipment preparation.

Pricing emergency services requires balancing fair compensation with customer needs during stressful situations. Understanding emergency service cost factors, including after hours labor rates and emergency material sourcing, helps establish appropriate pricing structures. Knowledge of insurance claim procedures and documentation requirements helps customers manage emergency expenses.

Training for emergency response should include regular practice of common scenarios, equipment familiarization, and procedure reviews. Understanding local emergency services coordination, including fire department and utility company protocols, improves response effectiveness. Regular updates on new equipment and techniques helps maintain emergency response capabilities.

The emotional aspects of emergency response require particular attention. Dealing with distressed customers, managing high stress situations, and maintaining professional composure while working under pressure demands specific skills. Understanding stress management techniques and maintaining appropriate work life balance helps sustain long term emergency response capability.

Success in emergency response and repair work ultimately depends on combining technical expertise, quick thinking, and professional judgment with careful attention to safety and customer needs. This challenging aspect of plumbing work offers opportunities to provide particularly valuable service while building strong customer relationships and professional reputation.

Reading Blueprints

Customer service represents a crucial aspect of success in the plumbing profession that extends far beyond technical expertise. While mechanical skills and problem solving abilities form the foundation of plumbing work, the ability to effectively interact with customers often determines long term professional success and business growth.

Professional plumbers must develop strong interpersonal skills to establish trust with customers from the first interaction. This begins with telephone communication, where plumbers need to gather accurate information about problems while reassuring anxious customers. Speaking clearly, asking relevant questions, and providing realistic timelines helps set appropriate expectations from the start.

First impressions upon arrival at a customer's property carry particular importance. Professional appearance, including clean uniforms and well maintained vehicles, helps establish credibility. Introducing oneself properly, listening carefully to customer concerns, and demonstrating respect for customer property creates positive initial interactions that support successful service delivery.

Explaining technical issues to customers who lack plumbing knowledge requires special communication skills. Professional plumbers learn to translate complex technical concepts into understandable terms without being condescending. Using simple analogies, clear explanations, and visual demonstrations helps customers understand problems and proposed solutions. This understanding supports informed decision making about repair options.

Providing accurate cost estimates and explaining pricing structures requires both technical knowledge and customer service skills. Professional plumbers must clearly communicate labor costs, material expenses, and potential complications that could affect final pricing.

Understanding customer budget constraints while maintaining profitable operations demands careful balance.

Working in customer homes requires particular sensitivity to privacy and property concerns. Professional plumbers develop protocols for protecting floors, furniture, and belongings while performing necessary work. Understanding and respecting cultural differences, personal preferences, and household routines helps maintain positive customer relationships throughout service delivery.

Documentation and communication about completed work helps prevent future misunderstandings. Professional plumbers provide detailed invoices explaining work performed, materials used, and warranty coverage. Taking time to review completed work with customers, demonstrate proper operation of new fixtures or equipment, and answer questions helps ensure customer satisfaction.

Handling customer complaints or concerns requires special attention to maintaining professional composure while addressing legitimate issues. Understanding common customer concerns, maintaining detailed work records, and developing fair resolution procedures helps manage difficult situations effectively. Following up after complaint resolution helps rebuild damaged customer relationships.

Emergency situations demand particularly careful attention to customer service. Professional plumbers must balance technical urgency with customer anxiety during high stress situations. Clear communication about immediate actions needed, potential complications, and ongoing work requirements helps customers cope with difficult circumstances.

Building long term customer relationships through excellent service creates valuable business advantages. Satisfied customers provide referrals, leave positive reviews, and return for future service needs. Understanding customer service as an investment in business growth rather than just an obligation helps guide professional conduct.

Modern communication technologies create new customer service opportunities and challenges. Professional plumbers must manage email communications, text messages, online reviews, and social media interactions while maintaining appropriate professional boundaries. Understanding which communications channels work best for different types of customer interaction helps optimize service delivery.

Commercial customers often have specific service requirements and expectations. Professional plumbers working with business clients must understand scheduling constraints, minimize business disruption, and coordinate with multiple stakeholders. Knowledge of commercial customer priorities helps guide service delivery in these settings.

Property management companies and institutional customers typically establish specific service protocols and documentation requirements. Professional plumbers working with these customers must understand work order systems, approval procedures, and reporting requirements. Maintaining positive relationships with both property managers and end users demands careful attention to established procedures.

Senior citizens and customers with special needs often require additional service considerations. Professional plumbers develop appropriate communication strategies, take extra time when needed, and ensure work areas remain safe and accessible. Understanding common concerns of various customer groups helps guide service delivery.

Cultural awareness and sensitivity increasingly affects customer service success. Professional plumbers working in diverse communities benefit from understanding cultural preferences, communication styles, and business practices. Respecting cultural differences while maintaining consistent professional standards helps build broad customer relationships.

Customer education about preventive maintenance and proper system operation represents an important service aspect. Professional plumbers who take time to explain maintenance requirements, demonstrate proper fixture operation, and answer customer questions build valuable long term relationships. Understanding customer education as an investment in future business helps guide service delivery.

Managing customer expectations throughout service delivery requires ongoing attention. Professional plumbers learn to provide realistic timelines, explain potential complications, and communicate clearly about work progress. Understanding how unmet expectations damage customer relationships helps guide professional conduct.

Service pricing discussions demand particular customer service skills. Professional plumbers must explain costs clearly while demonstrating value provided. Understanding customer budget constraints while maintaining profitable operations requires careful balance of business and customer service priorities.

Documentation of customer interactions helps prevent future misunderstandings and supports quality service delivery. Professional plumbers maintain detailed records of customer communications, work performed, and follow up requirements. Understanding documentation as a customer service tool rather than just a business requirement helps guide record keeping.

Ultimately, success in plumbing requires viewing customer service as an essential professional skill rather than an optional addition to technical expertise. The most successful plumbing professionals combine mechanical ability with strong interpersonal skills to build lasting customer relationships that support business growth and professional satisfaction.

Working with Schematics

Communication and professional conduct form essential pillars of success in the plumbing trade, going far beyond technical expertise to shape how others perceive and interact with plumbing professionals. This chapter explores the crucial elements of effective communication and maintaining professional standards throughout one's plumbing career.

Professional communication begins with understanding your audience. When speaking with customers, clear and accessible language proves far more effective than technical jargon. While you may understand the intricacies of a backflow preventer or the specifics of hydraulic gradient, your customers likely do not. Learning to translate complex plumbing concepts into everyday terms helps build trust and understanding with clients.

Written communication skills have become increasingly important in modern plumbing work. Professional plumbers must compose clear emails, write detailed work orders, and prepare comprehensive estimates. These documents often become legal records, making accuracy and clarity paramount. Taking time to proofread written communications and ensure all necessary information is included helps prevent misunderstandings and potential disputes.

Body language and nonverbal communication significantly impact professional interactions. Maintaining eye contact, offering a firm handshake, and demonstrating attentive listening through appropriate facial expressions and posture helps establish credibility. Professional plumbers learn to project confidence without appearing arrogant, showing respect for customers while demonstrating expertise.

Professional conduct extends to personal appearance and presentation. Clean, well maintained uniforms, proper grooming, and attention to personal hygiene create positive first impressions. While plumbing work inevitably involves getting dirty, starting each day with a professional appearance shows respect for customers and the trade.

Vehicle maintenance and organization also reflect professional standards. Clean, well maintained service vehicles with organized tool storage demonstrate attention to detail and professional pride. Understanding that your vehicle serves as a moving billboard for your professional reputation helps guide maintenance and presentation decisions.

Workplace conduct requires careful attention to professional boundaries. While friendly interaction builds customer relationships, maintaining appropriate professional distance prevents misunderstandings. Learning to be personable while remaining professional helps navigate various social situations encountered during plumbing work.

Time management represents another crucial aspect of professional conduct. Arriving on schedule, providing realistic time estimates, and communicating clearly about delays demonstrates respect for customer time. Understanding that punctuality and reliability directly impact professional reputation helps guide scheduling decisions.

Professional conduct includes appropriate use of technology during work hours. While mobile devices prove essential for modern plumbing work, personal phone use during customer interactions appears unprofessional. Establishing clear protocols for necessary work communications while avoiding distractions helps maintain professional standards.

Interaction with other trades requires particular attention to professional conduct. Construction sites often involve multiple contractors working in close proximity. Maintaining positive professional relationships while protecting customer interests demands careful balance. Understanding common courtesies and job site protocols helps prevent conflicts.

Professional conduct during bidding and estimation requires careful attention to ethical standards. Providing accurate, detailed estimates while maintaining competitive pricing demands honesty and transparency. Understanding how pricing decisions affect both customer relationships and industry reputation helps guide business practices.

Emergency situations test professional conduct under pressure. Maintaining calm demeanor while addressing urgent problems helps reassure anxious customers. Understanding how professional conduct during crisis situations impacts customer confidence helps guide behavior under stress.

Workplace safety demonstrates professional responsibility toward both customers and colleagues. Following established safety protocols, using appropriate protective equipment, and maintaining clean work areas shows professional commitment to workplace welfare. Understanding safety as an essential aspect of professional conduct helps guide daily work practices.

Professional conduct includes appropriate handling of confidential information. Customer financial details, property access codes, and observed household conditions require discrete management. Understanding privacy obligations helps build trust with customers while protecting professional reputation.

Environmental responsibility increasingly affects professional conduct standards. Proper disposal of materials, water conservation awareness, and attention to environmental regulations demonstrates professional commitment to sustainability. Understanding environmental impact of plumbing work helps guide professional practices.

Professional development through continuing education shows commitment to maintaining high standards. Staying current with new technologies, techniques, and regulations demonstrates professional dedication. Understanding how ongoing learning supports professional conduct helps guide career development.

Mentoring apprentices and new professionals requires modeling appropriate conduct standards. Demonstrating professional behavior while teaching technical skills helps maintain high industry standards. Understanding responsibility for developing future professionals helps guide interaction with learners.

Professional conduct extends to online presence and social media activity. Understanding how personal social media posts might affect professional reputation helps guide online behavior. Maintaining appropriate professional image across various platforms supports business success.

Industry association participation provides opportunities to demonstrate professional leadership. Active involvement in professional organizations shows commitment to advancing industry standards. Understanding how professional conduct within industry groups affects broader reputation helps guide participation.

Ultimately, communication skills and professional conduct represent fundamental requirements for long term success in plumbing. Technical expertise alone cannot overcome poor communication or unprofessional behavior. Understanding these skills as essential professional tools rather than optional additions helps guide career development and business growth.

Customer Service Skills

Time management and organizational skills form the bedrock of success in the plumbing trade, where efficiency directly impacts both customer satisfaction and business profitability. This chapter explores essential strategies for managing time effectively and maintaining organized work practices throughout a plumbing career.

Successful plumbers understand that each day requires careful planning to maximize productivity. The morning routine typically begins with reviewing scheduled appointments, organizing necessary tools and materials, and planning efficient travel routes between job sites. Taking time to prepare properly at the start of each day prevents costly delays and return trips for forgotten equipment.

Job scheduling demands particular attention to realistic time estimation. Experience teaches plumbers to account for various factors that influence job duration, including access challenges, parts availability, and potential complications. While customers appreciate quick service, underpromising and overdelivering proves more effective than optimistic scheduling that leads to delays.

Organization of service vehicles significantly impacts daily efficiency. Successful plumbers develop systematic approaches to tool and material storage, ensuring frequently used items remain easily accessible. Regular vehicle inventory checks help maintain appropriate stock levels while preventing time lost searching for misplaced tools or materials.

Documentation systems require careful organization to support efficient operations. Whether using paper records or digital solutions, maintaining organized customer files, work orders, and maintenance records proves essential. Establishing consistent filing systems helps quickly locate necessary information while ensuring important details don't slip through cracks.

Parts management presents unique organizational challenges. Successful plumbers develop systems for tracking inventory, organizing common replacement parts, and managing specialty items. Understanding which parts to stock in service vehicles versus store in shop inventory helps balance convenience against carrying costs.

Project management skills help organize complex plumbing installations or renovations. Breaking larger projects into manageable phases, coordinating with other trades, and maintaining clear timelines helps prevent costly delays. Understanding how to sequence work efficiently while maintaining quality standards requires careful organization.

Emergency response preparation demands particular attention to organization. Having systems in place for managing urgent calls while maintaining scheduled work helps balance competing demands. Successful plumbers develop strategies for prioritizing emergencies without completely disrupting planned activities.

Digital tools increasingly support time management and organization in modern plumbing work. Calendar applications, routing software, and inventory management systems help streamline operations. Learning to effectively utilize available technology while maintaining backup systems helps optimize efficiency.

Customer communication benefits from organized approaches. Maintaining clear records of customer preferences, property access details, and specific requirements helps provide consistent service. Organizing customer information in easily accessible formats supports efficient operations while improving service quality.

Financial organization proves essential for business success. Maintaining organized records of expenses, invoices, and payments helps manage cash flow effectively. Understanding how proper financial organization supports business planning and growth helps guide system development.

Time blocking helps manage various responsibilities effectively. Successful plumbers learn to allocate specific times for different activities, from customer appointments to administrative tasks. Understanding how to protect time for important but non urgent activities helps maintain balanced operations.

Warranty and maintenance tracking requires systematic organization. Maintaining clear records of installation dates, warranty terms, and scheduled maintenance helps prevent oversight. Understanding how organized tracking systems support customer service helps guide record keeping practices.

Tool maintenance benefits from organized approaches. Establishing regular maintenance schedules, tracking repair needs, and managing replacement cycles helps prevent equipment failures. Understanding how proper tool organization supports efficiency helps guide maintenance practices.

Supply chain management requires careful organization to prevent delays. Developing relationships with multiple suppliers, maintaining organized ordering systems, and tracking delivery schedules helps ensure material availability. Understanding how proper supply organization supports project completion helps guide purchasing practices.

Continuing education and certification renewal demand organizational attention. Tracking requirements, maintaining training records, and planning professional development activities helps prevent certification lapses. Understanding how organized approaches to professional development support career advancement helps guide learning activities.

Employee management requires systematic organization. Maintaining clear records of assignments, training completion, and performance reviews helps develop effective teams. Understanding how proper organization supports staff development helps guide management practices.

Code compliance benefits from organized approaches. Maintaining current references, tracking changes, and organizing inspection records helps ensure regulatory compliance. Understanding how proper organization supports legal compliance helps guide documentation practices.

Personal time management proves equally important as professional organization. Successful plumbers develop strategies for balancing work demands against personal needs. Understanding how proper organization supports work life balance helps guide scheduling decisions.

Ultimately, effective time management and organization represent essential skills for plumbing success. Technical expertise alone cannot overcome poor organization or inefficient time management. Understanding these skills as fundamental requirements rather than optional additions helps guide professional development and business growth.

Working with Clients

Working in different weather conditions presents unique challenges and considerations for plumbers who must maintain productivity and safety standards regardless of environmental factors. Understanding how to adapt work practices while maintaining quality proves essential for year round success in the plumbing trade.

Extreme heat creates particular challenges for plumbers working in attics, crawl spaces, and outdoor locations. High temperatures increase physical strain while reducing stamina and mental focus. Successful plumbers learn to schedule temperature sensitive work during cooler morning hours when possible, maintain proper hydration, and take regular cooling breaks. Using fans for ventilation, wearing appropriate lightweight clothing, and monitoring for heat stress symptoms helps maintain safety during hot weather work.

Cold weather introduces different complications for plumbing work. Frozen pipes, difficult ground conditions, and exposure risks require careful planning and preparation. Understanding how different materials respond to extreme cold, protecting exposed plumbing, and maintaining proper personal protection helps manage winter challenges. Carrying additional safety equipment, allowing extra time for weather related complications, and maintaining emergency supplies proves essential during cold weather operations.

Rain and wet conditions impact both outdoor and indoor plumbing work. Proper preparation includes maintaining waterproof tool storage, using appropriate protective equipment, and understanding how moisture affects different materials and procedures. Additional safety precautions become necessary when working with electrical tools in wet conditions. Managing muddy work sites, protecting open excavations, and maintaining safe access requires careful attention during wet weather.

Wind creates particular challenges for rooftop work, material handling, and maintaining stable work positions. Understanding wind load effects on equipment, securing materials properly, and maintaining additional safety measures helps manage these conditions. Communication may require adjustment during high winds, particularly when coordinating with other workers or operating equipment.

Lightning risk requires specific safety protocols, particularly during outdoor work or when operating metallic equipment. Understanding proper shutdown procedures, maintaining weather monitoring, and coordinating crew safety takes priority during electrical storms. Having clear evacuation procedures and designated shelter locations helps protect workers during dangerous conditions.

Seasonal changes impact scheduling and work planning throughout the year. Understanding how weather patterns affect different types of plumbing work helps optimize scheduling. Maintaining flexibility to adjust work sequences based on weather forecasts while keeping projects on track requires careful planning. Some specialized work may need scheduling during specific seasonal windows for optimal results.

Underground work faces particular weather related challenges. Soil conditions change significantly with weather variations, affecting excavation stability and work safety. Understanding how different weather conditions impact ground stability, maintaining appropriate shoring practices, and adjusting work methods helps manage these variations safely.

Weather considerations extend beyond immediate work conditions to impact material handling and storage. Some materials require specific temperature ranges for proper installation or storage. Understanding how weather affects different plumbing materials, maintaining appropriate storage conditions, and adjusting work practices helps ensure quality results.

Emergency response work often involves the most challenging weather conditions, as severe weather frequently triggers plumbing emergencies. Maintaining proper emergency equipment, understanding specific weather related risks, and following appropriate safety protocols becomes particularly important during difficult conditions. Having backup plans for various weather scenarios helps maintain emergency response capabilities.

Vehicle operations require additional attention during adverse weather. Maintaining proper vehicle equipment, adjusting driving practices, and allowing extra travel time helps manage transportation safely. Understanding how weather affects different vehicle systems, maintaining appropriate maintenance schedules, and carrying emergency supplies helps prevent weather related transportation problems.

Customer properties require particular protection during adverse weather conditions. Using appropriate barriers, maintaining cleanup procedures, and protecting finished surfaces from weather related damage helps maintain customer satisfaction. Understanding how different weather conditions affect various property protection methods helps guide appropriate precautions.

Tool and equipment maintenance becomes particularly important during challenging weather conditions. Understanding how weather affects different tools, maintaining appropriate cleaning and storage practices, and performing regular maintenance helps prevent weather related equipment failures. Carrying backup equipment for weather sensitive components helps maintain productivity during difficult conditions.

Personal protective equipment requirements often increase during adverse weather conditions. Understanding how different weather conditions affect various safety equipment, maintaining appropriate gear selection, and ensuring proper fit and function helps maintain worker protection. Regular inspection and maintenance of weather specific safety equipment helps ensure reliability when needed.

Ultimately, successful plumbers develop comprehensive strategies for maintaining safe and productive operations across all weather conditions. Understanding weather as a fundamental work factor rather than an occasional inconvenience helps guide appropriate preparation and response. Maintaining flexibility while ensuring consistent quality and safety standards requires careful attention to weather related factors throughout plumbing operations.

Marketing Your Plumbing Services

Gas fitting represents one of the most specialized and safety critical aspects of the plumbing trade. Working with natural gas and propane systems requires additional training, licensing, and strict adherence to safety protocols beyond standard plumbing work. The potential hazards of gas systems demand exceptional attention to detail and thorough understanding of proper installation and maintenance procedures.

Gas plumbers must develop comprehensive knowledge of different fuel gases and their properties. Natural gas and propane have distinct characteristics that affect system design, installation requirements, and safety considerations. Understanding gas pressures, flow rates, and combustion properties proves essential for proper system sizing and operation. Gas plumbers learn to calculate proper pipe sizes, pressure drops, and ventilation requirements to ensure safe and efficient system performance.

The installation of gas piping systems follows specific codes and standards developed to ensure public safety. Gas plumbers must understand and apply these requirements precisely, including proper pipe materials, joining methods, and testing procedures. System design must account for proper sizing, support, protection, and accessibility while maintaining required clearances and ventilation. Proper installation of shutoff valves, pressure regulators, and safety devices proves critical for system safety.

Testing and verification procedures for gas systems require particular attention and documentation. Gas plumbers must properly pressure test all new installations and repairs using appropriate test media and procedures. Understanding proper test pressures, duration requirements, and documentation helps ensure system integrity. Regular inspection and testing of existing systems helps maintain safety through early problem detection.

Gas appliance installation requires detailed knowledge of different equipment types and their specific requirements. Understanding proper venting, combustion air, and clearance requirements for various appliances helps ensure safe operation. Gas plumbers must properly size gas lines, verify proper pressure and flow rates, and confirm proper appliance operation after installation. Maintaining proper documentation of installations and testing helps verify compliance with safety requirements.

Troubleshooting gas systems demands systematic approaches and careful attention to safety. Gas plumbers learn to use proper leak detection methods, pressure testing procedures, and diagnostic equipment to identify problems safely. Understanding common failure modes, proper repair procedures, and system verification methods helps maintain safety during repairs. Emergency response procedures for gas leaks require particular attention to safety protocols and proper coordination with emergency services.

Ventilation systems play a critical role in gas system safety. Gas plumbers must understand proper sizing and installation of combustion air supplies and venting systems for different applications. Calculating proper vent sizes, maintaining proper clearances, and ensuring proper draft helps prevent dangerous conditions. Understanding how building modifications can affect ventilation systems helps maintain safety over time.

Carbon monoxide safety requires particular attention when working with gas systems. Gas plumbers must understand proper carbon monoxide detection methods, testing procedures, and safety devices. Proper installation and maintenance of carbon monoxide detectors helps protect building occupants. Understanding how different conditions can create carbon monoxide risks helps guide proper preventive measures.

Commercial and industrial gas systems present additional complexity and safety considerations. Higher pressures, larger systems, and specialized equipment require additional knowledge and precautions. Understanding proper installation and maintenance requirements for commercial equipment helps ensure safe operation. Coordination with other trades and careful attention to safety procedures becomes particularly important in commercial settings.

Gas system maintenance programs help prevent problems through regular inspection and testing. Gas plumbers develop systematic approaches to system evaluation, documentation, and preventive maintenance. Understanding common deterioration patterns, proper inspection methods, and appropriate maintenance procedures helps maintain system safety. Regular testing of safety devices and control systems helps ensure proper operation.

Emergency response procedures for gas systems require careful preparation and coordination. Gas plumbers must understand proper shutdown procedures, evacuation requirements, and coordination with emergency services. Maintaining proper emergency equipment, understanding specific hazard responses, and following established protocols helps manage gas emergencies safely. Regular review and practice of emergency procedures helps maintain response capabilities.

Documentation requirements for gas work exceed typical plumbing standards due to safety implications. Gas plumbers must maintain detailed records of installations, testing, and repairs to demonstrate compliance with safety requirements. Understanding proper documentation methods, maintaining appropriate forms and certificates, and following required reporting procedures helps ensure compliance. Proper record keeping helps verify system safety over time.

Continuing education proves particularly important for gas plumbers due to evolving technologies and safety requirements. Understanding new equipment types, installation methods, and safety requirements helps maintain current capabilities. Regular review of code updates, safety bulletins, and technical information helps maintain knowledge currency. Participation in industry training programs helps develop new skills and maintain certifications.

The increasing use of gas appliances in residential and commercial applications creates growing demand for qualified gas plumbers. Understanding current trends, new technologies, and evolving safety requirements helps maintain professional capabilities. Maintaining proper licensing, insurance, and certifications helps meet increasing customer expectations for gas system safety and reliability.

Gas plumbing represents one of the most challenging and rewarding specialties within the plumbing trade. The combination of technical knowledge, safety awareness, and attention to detail required for gas work demands exceptional professional commitment. Successful gas plumbers develop comprehensive understanding of systems, safety requirements, and proper procedures while maintaining constant focus on public safety through proper installation and maintenance practices.

Managing Finances and Bookkeeping

Water heaters represent a core component of modern plumbing systems, requiring specialized knowledge and skills to properly install, maintain, and repair these essential appliances. Understanding the various types of water heaters, their operation principles, and safety requirements proves crucial for plumbers working in both residential and commercial settings.

Storage tank water heaters remain the most common type, utilizing either gas or electric power for heating. These systems require careful sizing calculations to ensure adequate hot water supply while maintaining energy efficiency. Proper installation includes understanding clearance requirements, ventilation needs, and safety device operation. Temperature and pressure relief valve installation and testing demands particular attention to prevent dangerous conditions.

Tankless water heaters continue growing in popularity due to their energy efficiency and space saving benefits. These systems require detailed knowledge of proper sizing, venting requirements, and water quality considerations. Understanding flow rates, temperature rise calculations, and proper pipe sizing helps ensure adequate performance. Installation requires careful attention to manufacturer specifications and local code requirements.

Heat pump water heaters offer increasing efficiency advantages in appropriate applications. These systems require understanding of proper location requirements, air flow needs, and condensate management. Proper sizing calculations must account for both water heating needs and environmental conditions. Installation requires coordination of both plumbing and electrical components while maintaining proper clearances.

Solar water heating systems present unique installation and maintenance challenges. Understanding proper collector placement, system sizing, and freeze protection proves essential for successful installation. Proper integration with conventional backup systems helps ensure reliable operation. Maintenance requirements include regular inspection of components and proper fluid management.

Commercial water heating systems demand particular attention to sizing and safety requirements. Understanding peak demand calculations, storage requirements, and proper system configuration helps ensure adequate performance. Proper installation of recirculation systems, mixing valves, and safety devices proves critical for safe operation. Regular maintenance helps maintain system efficiency and reliability.

Water quality considerations significantly affect water heater operation and longevity. Understanding local water conditions, proper treatment methods, and maintenance requirements helps prevent premature failure. Regular flushing procedures, anode rod inspection, and scale prevention measures help maintain system efficiency. Proper documentation of maintenance activities helps track system condition over time.

Temperature control systems require careful attention during installation and maintenance. Understanding proper thermostat operation, mixing valve requirements, and temperature limitations helps ensure safe operation. Regular testing of control systems and safety devices helps prevent dangerous conditions. Proper adjustment and maintenance of recirculation systems helps maintain efficient operation.

Troubleshooting water heater problems demands systematic diagnostic approaches. Understanding common failure modes, proper testing procedures, and repair requirements helps resolve problems efficiently. Proper use of test equipment, careful documentation, and verification of repairs helps ensure safe operation. Emergency response procedures require particular attention to safety protocols.

Energy efficiency considerations increasingly influence water heater selection and installation. Understanding efficiency ratings, proper sizing methods, and insulation requirements helps optimize system performance. Proper installation of heat traps, pipe insulation, and control systems helps maintain efficiency. Regular maintenance helps prevent efficiency degradation over time.

Code compliance requires careful attention during water heater installation and replacement. Understanding proper support requirements, seismic restraints, and safety device installation helps ensure compliance. Proper permits, inspections, and documentation helps verify proper installation. Regular review of code updates helps maintain current knowledge.

Gas water heater installation requires additional safety considerations beyond standard plumbing work. Understanding proper gas line sizing, ventilation requirements, and safety device operation proves essential. Regular inspection and testing of gas components helps maintain safe operation. Emergency shutdown procedures require particular attention to safety protocols.

Electric water heater installation demands proper coordination with electrical systems. Understanding proper wire sizing, circuit requirements, and safety procedures helps ensure safe installation. Proper grounding, bonding, and overcurrent protection proves essential for safe operation. Regular inspection of electrical components helps maintain system safety.

Replacement installations present particular challenges in existing buildings. Understanding proper sizing, venting modifications, and code updates helps ensure successful installation. Proper management of confined spaces, access requirements, and safety procedures proves essential. Coordination with other trades often proves necessary for successful completion.

Water heater maintenance programs help prevent problems through regular inspection and service. Understanding manufacturer requirements, proper testing procedures, and preventive measures helps maintain reliable operation. Regular documentation of maintenance activities helps track system condition. Customer education regarding proper operation and maintenance helps prevent problems.

The increasing complexity of modern water heating systems demands ongoing professional development. Understanding new technologies, efficiency requirements, and safety standards helps maintain current capabilities. Regular review of technical information, participation in training programs, and maintenance of certifications helps ensure professional competence in this essential aspect of plumbing work.

Staying Up-to-Date with Industry Standards

Bathroom remodeling represents one of the most comprehensive and rewarding specializations within the plumbing trade, requiring a unique combination of technical expertise, design understanding, and project management skills. Successful bathroom remodeling projects demand careful planning, precise execution, and close coordination with other trades to deliver the functional and aesthetic results clients expect.

The planning phase of bathroom remodeling begins with a thorough assessment of existing conditions and client requirements. Understanding the current plumbing layout, structural limitations, and potential code compliance issues helps develop realistic project plans. Careful measurement and documentation of existing fixtures, pipe locations, and ventilation systems provides essential information for planning modifications. Discussion of client preferences, budget constraints, and timeline expectations helps establish clear project parameters.

Fixture selection and placement represents a critical aspect of bathroom remodeling projects. Understanding the space requirements, clearance needs, and installation specifications for various fixtures helps ensure proper layout decisions. Consideration of water supply requirements, drainage configurations, and venting needs influences fixture placement options. Proper planning of shower areas, bathtub installations, and vanity locations helps optimize space utilization while maintaining code compliance.

Plumbing rough in work demands particular attention during bathroom remodeling projects. Understanding proper pipe sizing, layout requirements, and installation methods helps ensure reliable system performance. Careful coordination with other trades regarding wall framing, electrical work, and ventilation modifications proves essential. Proper installation of water supply lines, drain pipes, and vent connections helps prevent future problems.

Waterproofing represents a crucial aspect of bathroom remodeling, particularly in shower and tub areas. Understanding proper membrane installation, drain flashing requirements, and sealing methods helps prevent water damage. Careful attention to slope requirements, corner treatments, and penetration sealing proves essential for long term performance. Proper coordination with tile installation helps ensure effective water management.

Shower installation presents particular challenges in bathroom remodeling projects. Understanding proper base preparation, drain installation, and waterproofing requirements helps ensure reliable performance. Careful attention to valve installation, supply line configuration, and temperature control proves essential for safety and functionality. Proper installation of shower doors or enclosures requires coordination with other trades.

Bathtub installation demands careful attention to support requirements and plumbing connections. Understanding proper leveling methods, drain installation, and overflow configuration helps prevent problems. Careful coordination of supply line installation, valve placement, and access panel requirements proves essential. Proper sealing and caulking helps prevent water damage around tub installations.

Vanity and sink installation requires consideration of both plumbing and aesthetic requirements. Understanding proper mounting methods, drain configuration, and supply line installation helps ensure satisfactory results. Careful coordination with countertop installation and cabinet work proves essential. Proper installation of faucets, drain assemblies, and shutoff valves helps ensure reliable operation.

Toilet installation in remodeling projects often presents unique challenges. Understanding proper flange installation, wax ring replacement, and mounting requirements helps ensure proper function. Careful attention to clearance requirements, supply line installation, and proper venting proves essential. Proper sealing and caulking helps prevent water damage around toilet bases.

Ventilation requirements demand particular attention during bathroom remodeling. Understanding proper fan sizing, duct installation, and termination requirements helps ensure effective moisture control. Careful coordination with electrical work and roof penetrations proves essential. Proper installation of timer controls or humidity sensors helps optimize ventilation system operation.

Code compliance requires careful attention throughout bathroom remodeling projects. Understanding current requirements for fixture spacing, ventilation, and accessibility helps ensure proper installation. Careful attention to permit requirements, inspection scheduling, and documentation proves essential. Regular review of code updates helps maintain current knowledge of requirements.

Project management skills prove particularly important in bathroom remodeling work. Understanding proper scheduling, trade coordination, and material management helps ensure efficient project completion. Careful attention to dust control, protection of finished surfaces, and cleanup requirements proves essential. Regular communication with clients and other trades helps maintain project progress.

Quality control demands consistent attention during bathroom remodeling projects. Understanding proper testing procedures, inspection requirements, and documentation needs helps ensure satisfactory results. Careful attention to finish details, caulking quality, and fixture operation proves essential. Final cleanup and client orientation helps ensure customer satisfaction.

The complexity of modern bathroom fixtures and systems requires ongoing professional development. Understanding new technologies, installation methods, and materials helps maintain current capabilities. Regular review of manufacturer specifications, participation in training programs, and maintenance of certifications helps ensure professional competence in this specialized aspect of plumbing work.

Cost estimation represents a crucial skill for bathroom remodeling projects. Understanding material costs, labor requirements, and potential complications helps develop accurate proposals. Careful attention to scope definition, allowances, and change order procedures proves essential. Regular review of pricing and cost tracking helps maintain profitable operations in this specialized market.

Professional Development

Green plumbing technologies represent an increasingly important aspect of modern plumbing work, driven by growing environmental awareness and regulatory requirements for sustainable building practices. Understanding and implementing these technologies helps plumbers meet client demands while contributing to resource conservation and environmental protection.

Water efficiency stands as a cornerstone of green plumbing technologies. Modern fixtures and systems incorporate advanced design features that maintain performance while significantly reducing water consumption. Dual flush toilets, low flow faucets, and water efficient showerheads demonstrate how technology can provide effective solutions without compromising user experience. Understanding the proper selection and installation of these fixtures helps plumbers deliver sustainable solutions.

Greywater systems represent another significant advancement in green plumbing technology. These systems capture and treat water from sinks, showers, and washing machines for reuse in appropriate applications like landscape irrigation or toilet flushing. Understanding system design requirements, treatment methods, and local regulations regarding greywater use proves essential. Proper installation and maintenance of these systems helps ensure safe and effective operation.

Rainwater harvesting systems continue gaining popularity as a sustainable water source. These systems collect and store rainwater for various non potable applications, reducing demand on municipal water supplies. Understanding proper tank sizing, filtration requirements, and pump systems helps ensure reliable operation. Careful attention to local regulations, water quality requirements, and system maintenance proves essential for successful implementation.

Solar water heating systems represent a growing segment of green plumbing technology. These systems utilize solar energy to reduce or eliminate conventional energy use for water heating. Understanding proper collector placement, storage tank requirements, and control systems helps ensure effective operation. Careful attention to freeze protection, temperature control, and backup systems proves essential in various climate conditions.

Heat pump water heaters demonstrate significant energy efficiency improvements over conventional systems. These units extract heat from surrounding air to warm water, substantially reducing energy consumption. Understanding proper installation requirements, space considerations, and operating parameters helps ensure satisfactory performance. Regular maintenance and monitoring helps maintain optimal efficiency.

Tankless water heaters continue evolving with improved efficiency and control capabilities. Modern units provide hot water on demand while eliminating standby losses associated with storage tanks. Understanding proper sizing, venting requirements, and maintenance needs helps ensure reliable operation. Careful attention to water quality and scale prevention proves essential for long term performance.

Water filtration and treatment systems increasingly incorporate sustainable technologies. Understanding various filtration methods, treatment options, and maintenance requirements helps provide appropriate solutions for different applications. Careful attention to water quality testing, filter replacement schedules, and system monitoring proves essential for effective operation.

Smart irrigation systems represent another aspect of green plumbing technology. These systems utilize weather data, soil moisture sensors, and advanced controls to optimize water use in landscape applications. Understanding proper system design, component selection, and programming helps ensure efficient operation. Regular maintenance and adjustment helps maintain optimal performance as conditions change.

Leak detection systems have evolved significantly with new technology. Modern systems utilize various sensors and monitoring devices to identify and report potential problems before significant water waste occurs. Understanding proper sensor placement, system programming, and alert protocols helps ensure effective operation. Regular testing and maintenance helps maintain system reliability.

Energy recovery systems demonstrate increasing sophistication in commercial applications. These systems capture and reuse waste heat from various processes to improve overall efficiency. Understanding proper system design, equipment selection, and control requirements helps ensure effective implementation. Regular monitoring and maintenance helps maintain optimal performance.

Building automation systems increasingly incorporate plumbing system control and monitoring. Understanding integration requirements, communication protocols, and control strategies helps ensure effective system operation. Careful attention to sensor calibration, control programming, and system maintenance proves essential for reliable performance.

Water quality monitoring systems utilize advanced technology to ensure compliance with various standards. Understanding proper sensor selection, installation requirements, and calibration procedures helps ensure accurate monitoring. Regular maintenance and verification helps maintain reliable operation of these critical systems.

Certification programs for green plumbing technologies continue evolving with industry developments. Understanding various certification requirements, testing procedures, and maintenance protocols helps ensure professional competence. Regular participation in continuing education helps maintain current knowledge of emerging technologies.

Cost benefit analysis proves particularly important when implementing green plumbing technologies. Understanding initial costs, operating expenses, and potential savings helps develop appropriate recommendations for various applications. Careful attention to incentive programs, regulatory requirements, and return on investment helps justify sustainable solutions.

The field of green plumbing technology continues advancing rapidly with new innovations and improvements. Maintaining current knowledge through professional development, manufacturer training, and industry participation helps ensure capability to implement these important technologies. Regular review of emerging technologies, regulatory changes, and market developments helps maintain professional competence in this crucial aspect of modern plumbing work.

Networking in the Plumbing Industry

Water conservation has become increasingly critical as populations grow and climate change impacts water resources worldwide. Modern plumbing practices must incorporate effective conservation methods to help preserve this essential resource while meeting customer needs and regulatory requirements.

Low flow fixtures represent a fundamental approach to water conservation. Modern designs utilize various technologies to maintain performance while significantly reducing water consumption. Aerators introduce air into water streams to maintain perceived flow while using less water. Pressure compensating devices ensure consistent performance across varying supply conditions. Understanding proper selection and installation of these fixtures helps achieve optimal results.

Water pressure management plays a crucial role in conservation efforts. Excessive pressure not only wastes water but can damage fixtures and increase leak potential. Pressure reducing valves help maintain appropriate pressure levels throughout plumbing systems. Regular monitoring and adjustment ensures optimal operation while preventing waste.

Fixture retrofitting provides cost effective conservation opportunities in existing buildings. Simple modifications like installing aerators, replacing flush valves, or upgrading showerheads can achieve significant water savings. Understanding various retrofit options and their applications helps develop appropriate recommendations for different situations.

Leak detection and repair represents another essential conservation strategy. Even small leaks can waste substantial amounts of water over time. Regular system inspection, pressure testing, and prompt repair of identified leaks helps prevent unnecessary waste. Modern detection equipment helps locate hidden leaks before they cause significant problems.

Water metering and monitoring systems help identify consumption patterns and potential waste. Submetering individual units or processes provides detailed usage data for analysis. Understanding proper meter selection, installation requirements, and monitoring procedures helps ensure accurate measurement.

Irrigation system optimization offers significant conservation potential in landscape applications. Modern control systems utilize weather data and soil moisture sensors to prevent overwatering. Proper sprinkler selection and placement helps ensure efficient coverage. Regular system maintenance and adjustment maintains optimal performance.

Commercial kitchen applications present unique conservation opportunities. Pre rinse spray valves, water efficient dishwashers, and proper operating procedures help reduce consumption. Understanding equipment options and best practices helps develop effective conservation strategies.

Cooling tower operation significantly impacts water consumption in many facilities. Proper chemical treatment, blowdown control, and maintenance procedures help optimize water use while maintaining system performance. Understanding various efficiency improvements helps reduce consumption while maintaining reliable operation.

Process water recycling provides conservation opportunities in various applications. Understanding treatment requirements, system design, and operating parameters helps implement effective solutions. Regular monitoring and maintenance ensures reliable performance while maintaining water quality standards.

Educational programs play an important role in conservation efforts. Training building occupants and maintenance staff helps ensure proper system operation and prompt problem reporting. Understanding various educational approaches helps develop effective programs for different situations.

Water auditing procedures help identify conservation opportunities. Systematic evaluation of water using systems and processes reveals potential improvements. Understanding proper audit procedures and analysis methods helps develop effective recommendations.

Cost analysis proves essential when evaluating conservation measures. Understanding initial costs, potential savings, and available incentives helps justify improvements. Careful attention to return on investment helps prioritize various conservation options.

Regulatory requirements increasingly mandate water conservation measures. Understanding various codes and standards helps ensure compliance while achieving conservation goals. Regular review of regulatory changes helps maintain current knowledge of requirements.

Documentation and reporting procedures help track conservation progress. Recording baseline consumption, implemented measures, and achieved savings provides valuable data for future planning. Understanding proper documentation methods helps demonstrate program effectiveness.

Water conservation technology continues advancing with new innovations and improvements. Maintaining current knowledge through professional development and industry participation helps provide effective solutions. Regular review of emerging technologies and best practices helps maintain professional competence in this essential aspect of modern plumbing work.

Performance verification ensures conservation measures achieve intended results. Regular monitoring and adjustment helps maintain optimal efficiency. Understanding various verification methods helps demonstrate actual savings and identify potential improvements.

Long term planning helps develop comprehensive conservation strategies. Understanding facility needs, available technologies, and implementation priorities helps achieve sustainable results. Regular plan review and updates maintains program effectiveness as conditions change.

Maintaining Licenses and Certifications

Smart home integration represents an increasingly important aspect of modern plumbing as technology continues transforming residential and commercial buildings. Today's plumbers must understand how various smart systems interact with plumbing components to provide effective installation and service.

Smart water monitoring systems form a foundation of connected plumbing technology. These systems use sensors to track water flow, pressure, temperature and quality throughout buildings. When properly integrated, they can detect leaks, analyze usage patterns, and alert owners to potential problems before major damage occurs. Understanding sensor placement, calibration requirements, and communication protocols helps ensure reliable system operation.

Water heater controls have evolved significantly with smart technology integration. Modern systems allow remote temperature adjustment, usage scheduling, and maintenance monitoring. Some units can even learn occupant preferences and automatically adjust operation for optimal efficiency. Knowledge of various control options and their programming requirements helps provide appropriate solutions for different applications.

Fixture automation continues advancing with new capabilities. Smart faucets, toilets, and shower systems offer touchless operation, customized settings, and usage tracking. Voice control integration allows hands free operation in many applications. Understanding proper selection, installation requirements, and configuration procedures helps ensure customer satisfaction with these advanced systems.

Irrigation control systems now incorporate weather data, soil sensors, and automated scheduling. Smart controllers can adjust watering patterns based on current conditions and forecast data. Mobile connectivity allows remote monitoring and adjustment.

Knowledge of various control options and their programming helps optimize system performance while conserving water.

Whole house water management systems coordinate multiple smart components. These systems can monitor usage, adjust pressure, control temperature, and manage water treatment equipment. Some even integrate with home automation platforms for centralized control. Understanding system architecture and configuration requirements helps achieve proper integration.

Leak detection technology has advanced significantly with smart capabilities. Modern systems use multiple sensor types and sophisticated algorithms to identify potential problems. Automatic shut off valves can prevent major damage when leaks occur. Knowledge of various detection methods and their applications helps provide appropriate solutions.

Mobile connectivity plays a crucial role in smart plumbing systems. Smartphone apps allow remote monitoring and control of various components. Understanding network requirements, security considerations, and user interface options helps ensure reliable operation and positive user experience.

Data analytics capabilities continue expanding in smart plumbing applications. Advanced systems can analyze usage patterns, predict maintenance needs, and optimize system performance. Understanding data collection, analysis methods, and reporting options helps maximize system benefits.

Integration with building automation systems requires careful coordination. Smart plumbing components must communicate effectively with HVAC, lighting, and other building systems. Understanding various communication protocols and integration requirements helps ensure proper system operation.

Cybersecurity considerations have become increasingly important as systems become more connected. Proper network configuration, access control, and security updates help prevent unauthorized system access. Understanding various security measures and best practices helps protect sensitive systems and data.

Installation procedures for smart components often differ from traditional plumbing work. Additional wiring, network connections, and control system configuration may be required. Understanding proper installation sequences and testing procedures helps ensure reliable operation.

Troubleshooting smart systems requires both plumbing and technology knowledge. Problems may involve mechanical components, sensors, controls, or communication systems. Understanding various diagnostic procedures and common issues helps provide effective solutions.

User training plays an essential role in smart system success. Building owners and occupants must understand system operation and maintenance requirements. Knowledge of various training approaches helps develop effective programs for different situations.

Documentation requirements often expand with smart system installation. Network configurations, control parameters, and maintenance procedures must be properly recorded. Understanding documentation needs helps ensure long term system support.

Cost considerations impact smart technology adoption. Initial costs, potential savings, and available incentives influence implementation decisions. Understanding various cost factors helps develop appropriate recommendations for different situations.

Future trends indicate continued smart technology expansion in plumbing applications. New capabilities and integration options regularly emerge. Maintaining current knowledge through professional development helps provide effective solutions as technology advances.

Smart home integration represents a significant opportunity for plumbing professionals to expand their capabilities and provide enhanced value to customers. Success requires understanding both traditional plumbing principles and modern technology applications.

Regular learning and adaptation helps maintain professional competence as this field continues evolving.

Don't miss out!

Visit the website below and you can sign up to receive emails whenever Mike Turner publishes a new book. There's no charge and no obligation.

https://books2read.com/r/B-A-JEHUC-NYZHF

BOOKS 2 READ

Connecting independent readers to independent writers.

www.ingramcontent.com/pod-product-compliance
Lightning Source LLC
Chambersburg PA
CBHW020542160726
47991CB00002B/551